**New Challenges
to the Role of Profit**

The Diebold Institute for Public Policy Studies, Inc.

The John Diebold Lectures are made possible by a grant from The Diebold Institute for Public Policy Studies, Inc., an operating nonprofit foundation established in 1967 by John Diebold, Chairman and founder of The Diebold Group, Inc., management consultants. The Institute serves as a link between the public and private sectors on matters of public policy. It focuses its research on present and future market systems.

The Institute functions on the dual premise that those concerned, even indirectly, with bringing about the application of scientific and technological change should also concern themselves with the human and social implications of that change, and that society's response to this problem has been inadequate. The private nature of the needed response to what is essentially a public-policy problem is a basic consideration of the Institute's activities.

Among the programs initiated by the Institute is the development of a series of monographs on the social and managerial problems of technological change. Another program is the sponsorship of The John Diebold Lectures at Harvard University, a joint effort of the Department of Economics and the Graduate School of Business Administration, which seeks to bring to the Harvard community distinguished administrators of scientifically based enterprises to explore the interaction of technology and management. Another program is a research interchange arrangement in which more than one hundred research and academic institutions provide a review of ongoing research.

The first series of The John Diebold Lectures was presented at the Harvard Business School between 1968 and 1970. The second series was held on December 9, 1971, at The Hague. This third series was conducted in 1976 at Harvard University.

New Challenges to the Role of Profit

The Third Series of The John
Diebold Lectures at Harvard
University

Edited by

Benjamin M. Friedman
Harvard University

Lexington Books
D.C. Heath and Company
Lexington, Massachusetts
Toronto

Library of Congress Cataloging in Publication Data

Main entry under title:

New challenges to the role of profit.

   (The John Diebold lectures; 1976)
   1. Profit—Addresses, essays, lectures. I. Friedman, Benjamin M. II. Series.
HB601.N48   338.5'16   78-388
ISBN 0-669-02171-7

International Standard Book Number: 0-669-02171-7

Library of Congress Catalog Card Number: 78-388

Contents

Foreword

In February 1976 the third series of The John Diebold Lectures was held at Harvard University. The lectures were sponsored by the Department of Economics and funded by a generous gift from The Diebold Institute for Public Policy Studies. The subject was "New Challenges to the Role of Profit." This book makes available to the general public—the ultimate target of these lectures—the principal papers delivered on that occasion: the thoughts and speculations of Kenneth Arrow, Erik Lundberg, and Paul Samuelson. Summarized remarks by the discussants have also been included. My colleague Benjamin Friedman has edited the volume and contributed an introductory chapter.

The Diebold Lectures have always reflected the perspective and philosophy of their distinguished founder, John W. Diebold. The subjects of the two previous series were the relations between changing technology and management, and the interaction of science policy and business. Both of these topics were (and remain) timely and complex subjects, particularly suitable for discussion by various constituencies: businessmen, academics, public servants, interested laymen, and students.

Obviously the same is true for the lecture series presented in 1976. Western economics has always considered profits to be the necessary and legitimate return of enterprise. Most economists who have concerned themselves with economic growth and social development have stressed the crucial role of profits as an engine of progress. And yet it must be quite clear that both in the United States and abroad—in what we might loosely call capitalist countries—the legitimacy of profits is under increasing attack. When business profits become very large there frequently is the suggestion of something "wrong" from the public point of view. Sometimes we are urged to pursue wage and price controls. In many countries there have been experiments with worker participation in management. More important for our future, perhaps, it is my impression as a teacher that many of our best educated young people are disenchanted with the operation of market forces and with the system of distribution described and lauded in standard textbooks.

Therefore it is not surprising that large and interested audiences attended these lectures. There were business leaders and Harvard undergraduates, Washington bureaucrats and university professors, foreign visitors and union officials. Nearly everyone had questions and comments, and debate was lively. I hope that this book can convey a sense of these enjoyable meetings.

A number of people gave great help in making possible the lectures and their publication. My friend John Diebold was the "necessary condition" and we are all in his debt. He was ably assisted by Ralph Weindling of The Diebold Group. At Harvard, my thanks go especially to Ben Friedman, as well as to Alan

Auerbach. Lastly, my gratitude also goes to our most distinguished speakers, discussants, and audience. They made the third series of The Diebold Lectures a memorable occasion.

Henry Rosovsky
Dean of the Faculty of Arts and Sciences
Harvard University

New Challenges
to the Role of Profit

1 Profits and Challenges to Profits: An Introduction

Benjamin M. Friedman

Like most other widely debated aspects of society's arrangements, profits cut two ways—one applauded and one regretted. The role of profits that most people approve is the allocation of society's economic efforts and resources. The role to which many object is the distribution of society's rewards. On the one side, to make decisions about what and how much to produce, and how to produce it, advanced Western economies have evolved complex systems of which business profits are, at least in principle, an important and widely accepted element. At the same time, who gets how much of what depends in large part on the respective income and wealth of individuals.

If the distribution of rewards had no impact on the total amount of society's economic dividend—that is, if the profit motivation had no effect on people's effort—most people would prefer (or say they would prefer) that individuals receive roughly equal shares of it. But if reducing the role of business profits made the economy less efficient, either by lowering the overall level of effort or by altering its allocation, there would be fewer total rewards to distribute. Conversely, if the allocative system did not change the distribution of rewards, most people would favor whatever system was most efficient. But business profits tend on the whole to increase the inequality of incomes and wealth and hence of individuals' ability to draw on what society produces.

Debates about profits usually focus on these conflicting aspects of the role of profit in two ways. First, how effective is the role people approve, and how serious is the one they condemn? Do profits actually exert the motivating force which textbook treatments place at the core of the economic allocation mechanism? Or has the "mixing" of the economy—which meshes large corporations with pervasive government influence—already evolved alternative decision-making processes in which profits assume only an ancillary part? On the other side of the issue, do business profits continue to be a major determinant of the distribution of income and wealth? Or is the impact of profits small in comparison to redistributive programs like the progressive income tax and the Social Security System?

These are the questions that frame the descriptive side of debates about profits. The issues here are positive ones, about how modern Western economies work. By contrast, the second focus of discussions about profits is prescriptive. Are there ways to improve society's economic arrangements? In particular, is there a way of preserving—and perhaps even enhancing—the allocative role of business profits while blunting their distributive consequences? Alternatively, are there

1

wholly different ways of establishing the allocation of effort and resources that would be free of the distributional aspects of the profit system yet also be consistent with society's broader social and political ideals?

In the third series of The John Diebold Lectures, held at Harvard in 1976, Paul Samuelson, Kenneth Arrow, Erik Lundberg, and 13 other participants addressed the troubled prospects of profits in the modern economy. While their diverse treatments range broadly among different aspects of the subject—from Samuelson's review of the role of profits from the perspective of economic theory, to Arrow's inquiry into the moral and philosophical roots of attitudes toward profits and their consequences, to Lundberg's description of a particular means of redirecting the distribution of profits—each reflects the fundamental dilemma of the allocative and distributive roles of profits: How important are profits in deciding on economic allocations, and how well do they decide them? How serious are the resulting distributional inequalities? Is there a way to separate allocative and distributive effects of profits? What choices about the role of profits does society have within the current structure? Is there a better structure?

The major relevance of these questions to the current economics and politics of countries like the United States does not lie in the (presumably remote) possibility that society may some day undertake a broadly based rethinking of its long-standing arrangements. Instead these questions are vital because they impinge on a host of current policy issues for which the role of profits is a key determinant of the best policy choice. Would higher (possibly deregulated) oil and gas prices call forth greater domestic fuel supplies? Would reducing corporate income taxes, eliminating "double taxation" of corporate dividends, or abolishing the tax distinction between capital gains and ordinary income significantly encourage business investment in new plant and equipment? Would subsidizing research and development programs or guaranteeing the credit of some small companies accelerate the economy's rate of technological progress? Would restructuring the antitrust laws to permit American firms the same freedoms as their foreign competitors improve the nation's balance of trade? Would redesigning labor practice laws to change the balance of power between businesses and unions—for example, requiring some members of corporate boards of directors to represent unions or prohibiting unemployment and welfare payments to striking workers—either improve or exacerbate the economy's inflation problem?

Each of these issues is currently on the economic policy agenda of the United States, either in the broad sense of major legislation pertinent to the entire economy or in the narrower sense of specific regulatory, judicial, or executive decisions applicable to individual industries or even individual companies. In each case, the best policy to adopt depends, at least in part, on the role of business profits in the economic process. In each case, the view that profits are unimportant in business decision making (or that they should be unimportant) would lead to a different policy from that implied by a belief in the strength and value of profits. Each individual case, of course, has its particular merits on either side, wholly apart from the role of profits, and each individual policy decision is a far step from the kind of overview of the role of profits attempted in this set of lectures. Nevertheless, individual policy decisions in individual cases like these do, collectively, determine the evolution of the nation's economic system in the broadest sense.

Informed thinking about the role of profits therefore has a direct policy relevance—not simply for the specifics of individual policy issues, but also for the prospective evolution of the role of profits itself. In all probability, the major influence of such thinking on the role of profits in the large will come about through specific policy descriptions in the small.

Wrangles over easy questions resolve themselves rapidly. By contrast, the debate about the role of profits is as old as private enterprise. Indeed, in recent years it has appeared not to abate but to gain vigor, while evoking new challenges to the whole notion of the value of profits. The reason, of course, is that the important questions at issue—both descriptive and prescriptive—are extraordinarily difficult. Merely establishing the facts is a major challenge. In economic systems as complex as those of the industrialized West today, wholesale simplifications are necessary before one can even begin to think about what is happening; and the absence of anything remotely resembling laboratory study conditions renders strict application of the scientific method impossible. People with different "perspectives"—that is, people who have chosen to simplify in different ways by looking carefully at different pieces of the economy while assuming away the rest—naturally reach different conclusions, but there is then no ready way to evaluate their competing visions of economic reality. Similarly, the inability of economists (and, usually, of politicians) to perform controlled experiments on real people and firms not only complicates the job of discovering how the economy works, but renders nearly impossible any confident prediction of how adequately some new system for achieving society's economic ends would, if implemented, work in place of the current one.

The Role of Profits in Allocation

The role of business profits in influencing economic decisions is a subject to which economists turn again and again. The standard textbook view is that firms seek to make as much profit as possible within the constraints imposed by production technology (supply factors) and market conditions (demand factors). The great preponderance of scholarly research in economics also either implicitly or explicitly accepts this proposition, in order to provide a guide for determining firms' behavior. Businesses' striving after profits then explains, for example, why no company is currently producing pin heads engraved with verse from the Iliad (weak demand) and why no company is currently producing oil drawn from shale deposits (expensive supply). More precisely, both supply and demand are important in each instance. Some collectors would probably pay 1 cent each for Iliad pins if engravers could produce them that cheaply, but they can't. And energy companies would gladly melt shale into crude oil at a cost of $20 per barrel if refiners would pay that price for the crude, but they won't.

It is ultimately the motivation of profits that generates a response to the information provided by prices. There must be some reason *why* engravers will not make a pin for $10 and sell it for 1 cent, and *why* energy companies will not produce a barrel of shale oil for $20 and sell it for $12. The conventional answer is that a preference for profits instead of losses—and beyond that a preference for more profits instead of less—motivates the behavior of firms. Hence clothes manufacturers will produce this year's fashions rather than last year's, even though there may still be enough demand for the older styles to cover costs and show a modest profit. And light bulb manufacturers will use tungsten instead of silver filaments, even though the extra cost of the silver would not dissipate profits entirely.

After some extrapolation and refinement, this simple notion of *constrained profit maximization* as the prime mover of business behavior leads to a strongly appealing conception of economic efficiency. Markets place the correct marginal valuation on each natural resource or kind of labor, as well as on each produced good or service. And profit maximization leads businesses to use this wealth of information contained in prices to produce the amount and composition of final production which best satisfies the requirements and desires of society's members—individually weighted, of course, by their claims on that production as measured by their respective incomes and assets. Economic theorists have long disagreed about whether the rate of profit that each business could earn in the ultimate limit of this static conception would be positive or zero after appropriate adjustments for interest and other costs, but in either case the allocative force of the profit motive remains important for at least two reasons. First, even in the abstraction of an economy in which businesses had already bid away all positive profits en route to the efficient allocation of resources, the pressure to break even rather than make losses would still provide the motivation for companies to preserve that efficient allocation and not drift into different, less efficient activities. Second, and more important, an actual economy in fact never reaches *the* efficient allocation. Real economies are dynamic, not stationary, and the allocative role of profits in a dynamic setting is to motivate innovation in the form of new products, new methods of production, new markets, new sources of supply, and new industrial organizations. A reading of this set of lectures by today's leading economic theorists immediately suggests that the importance of profits for entrepreneurship and innovation, and hence for the dynamics of economic development, remains as central an issue today as when Joseph Schumpeter first emphasized it in the early years of this century.

While this familiar textbook version of the role of profits usually focuses on the allocation of resources among competing uses in current production—what goods to make, and how to make them—in a growing economy profits also play an important part in allocations over time. How much of the product of society's labors should its members enjoy now, and how much should they put aside to make production easier in the future? More concretely, how should the economy divide its production between consumption and investment goods? Since profits in today's frame of reference accrue primarily to owners of capital and of claims on capital, and indeed provide the primary incentive to new capital formation, the rising debate over the role of capital formation in economic growth and over appropriate policies toward capital formation inevitably becomes, at some level, a debate about the role of profits. The recent controversy about whether or not a permanent secular decline in profits (measured as a return to investment) has occurred in the U.S. economy during the past two decades, for example, assumes importance primarily because of the presumption that a lower profit rate will retard investment in productive plant and equipment and thereby impede progress in raising living standards.

In addition, as a result of the many imperfections that characterize even financial markets as well developed as those in the United States, business profits play a double role in the fixed-investment aspects of the economy's intertemporal allocations. Profits not only motivate investment, they help to finance it. While textbook models (and too many scholarly papers) assume that anonymous "capitalists" stand willing to lend a company whatever amount of funds it requires to finance its investments in new plant and equipment, simply charging whatever interest rate is appropriate for the riskiness of the intended project, in fact many companies behave as if their access to external funds from the financial markets is limited, and most companies behave as if the markets' supply of external funds is more expensive the more they tap it. Hence the often thin margin of funds internally generated and retained, representing profits net of both taxes and dividends, plays a special role in directly financing new investment as well as increasing the equity base against which a company may seek external funds from the financial markets.

In a growth context, the need to attract external funds from new investors, through implicit promises of future dividends, further bolsters the motivating force by which the desire to earn profits for current investors guides corporations' decisions. At the same time, the ability of investors to select where to place their new savings (or to replace their current dividends) means that the promise of future profits also guides the allocation of capital among different corporations, as well as between the corporate sector as a whole and alternative uses of saving like homebuilding.

Questioning the Allocative Role of Profits

How closely do these descriptions of the allocative role of profits, in determining both the uses of resources today and the division between their use today or in the future, resemble the reality of the modern mixed economy? Does the system actually work as advertised? This is the question—along with the distributional inequality that accompanies the use of the profit system—that lies at the core of the profits debate. There are two kinds of familiar reasoning against the allocative role of profits, and it is useful to distinguish between them because of their sharply different implications for public policy.

First, there exists an entire litany of arguments to the effect that the profit system does not work, or at least does not work well, because government has already interfered with it too much. In order to offset the distributional consequences of profits, the government taxes away most of the incentives. A large profit, diluted first by a 48 percent corporate income tax rate and next by a 70 percent personal income tax rate on the remainder, provides little motivation for allocating savings among different corporations, even before allowance for such matters as inheritance taxes on sums not consumed in one's own lifetime. Because it is unwilling to acknowledge the full implications of the inflation problem, the government taxes nominal profits even though such profits may really be losses after proper allowance for overall price increases. An investment paying 8 percent interest taxed at a 50 percent rate would have netted a negative real return over the past decade in the United States, as would a stock bought a decade ago at $100 and sold now at $200 subject to 35 percent capital gains tax plus the "minimum" tax on "preference" income. In order to eliminate harmful externalities which private decisions alone would not ordinarily prevent, the government has already so drastically shrunk the scope of private business decision making as to remove incentives. A clever invention which would allow auto producers to meet stricter safety, antipollution or gas-mileage standards while still making large profits would lead only to a further tightening of the imposed standards. In order to prevent widespread poverty among elderly citizens, the government provides unfunded retirement income guarantees that discourage genuinely funded private saving, as individuals put less money into the capital markets because Social Security owes them trillions of dollars while the Social Security Fund puts into the capital markets only a few billions out of these lost trillions. The list goes on.

A second kind of argument holds that, even apart from the influence of government, the profit system still does not serve its intended allocative function very well. Instead of accepting the proposition that businesses would indeed maximize profits if only the government would let them do so, the disagreement here is with the initial assumption of profit maximization itself. One version of this argument is that the operations of the large corporations which dominate the modern business world are so complicated that their managements cannot possibly maximize profits even if they unambiguously desire to do so. At best they can meet some less exacting criterion in which profits probably exert an important though far from unique influence. While profit maximization may continue to determine the allocation of capital *among* corporations therefore, the role of profits in determining *within*-corporation decisions is uncertain.

An alternative form of this argument questions whether a corporation's hired managers, who receive salaries and typically own only tiny fractions of the corporation's stock, even seek to behave so as to maximize the profits that accrue to its shareholders. Despite a variety of incentive-compensation schemes for corporate executives, the personal objectives of managers are unlikely to be precisely congruent with those of shareholders. In recent years, examples of shareholder suits against managements for opposing takeover bids well above the market value of the stock have vividly illustrated the nature of the potential conflicts. In addition, the convoluted and often deliberately obfuscated nature of the share ownership in most large corporations renders the concept of ultimate stockholder decision making little more than a legal fiction. Managers can always assume that some straightforward criterion (like profit maximization subject to a risk adjustment) fully summarizes the stockholders' preferences; but in most companies there is no practical way for the managers to find out what the shareholders do want even if they genuinely try to seek guidance. (Indeed, in one highly publicized recent situation involving bribery, it was only by losing his job that the chief executive officer of a major company discovered that the directors elected by his company's shareholders valued some factors more highly than profits; but in this case the crucial element was probably the corporation's atypical pattern of stock ownership, which involved an open holding of a large minority interest by a single family.)

It is useful to distinguish these two categories of objections to the allocative role of business profits, since their implications for policy usually differ markedly. If profits fail to motivate business toward an efficient allocation of the economy's resources because government has gotten in the way, then one plausible response is that government should get out of the way. In particular, government should then seek ways to accomplish public-policy objectives while minimizing the degree of unwanted distortion of private-sector decision making. Whether this response makes practical sense—or alternatively, whether the primacy of public goals inevitably reduces the allocative role of profits to a second-order influence not worth preserving—in principle remains an open question. By contrast, if the profit system fails to achieve efficient allocations because it is itself internally unworkable in the modern economy, then the appropriate policy response is unambiguously to declare the profit system not worth the associated distributional inequality.

The Role of Profits in Distribution

If assessing the evidence on the allocative role of profits has proven difficult, the question of the distributive impact of profits seems even more subject to basic contradictions and misperceptions.

In the United States, the federal government's "take" out of each dollar of gross national product has risen irregularly from 18 cents a generation ago to 23 cents today. During these years, the government's actual usage of goods and services, however, has shrunk as a fraction of the nation's total output (from over 12 cents in the dollar to less than 8), and so the entire source of the rising rather than falling relative size of federal government activity is the steady increase of transfer payments (from 3 cents in the dollar to 9). While the redistributive intention of some of these transfers is readily evident—food stamps, for example, or other welfare assistance—substantial confusions and even some popular mythology often cloud the recognition that other, larger government transfer programs also provide substantial redistribution. For example, although the popular image of the Social Security System is a savings-and-insurance scheme which returns to each individual a retirement income determined by the actuarially fair value of his or her contributions, in fact the system sets its benefits so as to make it in part a tax-and-transfer mechanism that redistributes income from higher wage earners to lower. Similarly, the unemployment insurance system gears contributions of companies to their work-experience ratings in a way that on balance combines a redistributive function with the familiar risk-sharing one.

The *federal* government, however, is the lesser part of the story of the sharp rise in the overall government share in the post-World War II era, since *state and local* governments have increased their "take" from 8 cents of each dollar of gross national product in the early 1950s to 14 cents today. In contrast to the federal government's pattern of declining usage of goods and services and sharply rising transfers, state and local governments have increased both their transfers (from 1 cent in the dollar to 3) and their purchases of goods and services (from 7 cents in the dollar to 13). Here again, untangling the redistributive effects associated with greatly increased expenditures on such facilities as schools and hospitals—financed about equally out of property taxes, sales taxes, personal income taxes, and grants from the federal government—is a challenging job.

An even greater apparent contradiction follows from comparing the respective distributions of incomes and wealth. Almost entirely because of the rapid growth of government transfer programs, the distribution of *incomes* in the United States today reflects significantly less inequality than was the case several decades ago. One estimate of the net effect of federal programs alone is that they served to raise more than 16 million people above the official poverty level in 1975. By contrast, most conventional measures of the distribution of *wealth* suggest no noticeable trend toward either greater or less inequality. These conventional measures, however, exclude that part of wealth which takes the form of claims against future pension benefits, especially from Social Security. The actuarial present value of the Social Security System's currently outstanding obligations to private citizens has grown faster than geometrically since the system's introduction some four decades ago, and it now totals several trillion dollars—about as much as the entirety of all other forms of privately held wealth. Given the relatively equal distribution of this "Social Security wealth" among individuals, including it in the concept of total holdings destroys the impression that the distribution of wealth has been stationary. Depending on which of several different estimates of Social Security wealth is included, in fact, the distribution of wealth may be evolving in the direction of equality even faster than the distribution of income. And, although it is too early to say with confidence, the recently enacted estate tax changes will probably further accelerate this trend.

Still, profits are not the only source of inequalities in income and wealth; and, in any debate on the role of profits, it is important to distinguish their contribution from that of unequal wages and other factors. Here, too, a host of contradictions and misperceptions plagues most attempts to discuss the issues. In recent years the share of profits in total U.S. national income has declined by and large, and so has the rate of profit on the economy's total business investment (although here a partial reversal has occurred in just the past few years). Many people have accepted this pattern of declining profits as an immediate sign of a sharply eroding role of profits in the economy. A large part of this decline merely reflects the typical company's move toward greater debt and reduced equity financing, which naturally results in more interest and less profits as shares of the total return on the company's investment, so that simply to focus on reported profit ratios is hardly adequate to the task at hand. Even so, after allowances for the shift from profits to interest and for other similarly offsetting items, it remains true that profits are proportionally smaller, and therefore potentially less damaging to the distribution of income and wealth (though perhaps also less able to serve their allocative purpose) than was the case in previous years.

In addition, the public perception does usually overestimate the magnitude of profits, although the profits-to-sales ratio emphasized in a number of recent opinion surveys hardly seems relevant in light of its dependence both on the degree of vertical integration in the economic structure and on the sales-to-capital ratio of individual businesses. Profits totaling 3 percent of sales mean something very different in a service business, for example, in which there are few material inputs for the company to buy or facilities to maintain, than in the supermarket business, in which expenses consist mostly of the cost of goods purchased (and, to a lesser extent, facilities maintained). Even in the manufacturing and processing industries, the same profits-to-sales ratio may be large or small depending on the company's purchases of intermediate goods. A business in which the product changes hands many times on its way to the final consumer will naturally have a lower profits-to-sales ratio than a vertically integrated business which begins with raw materials and delivers a finished product. What matters for any company from this perspective is not its profits-to-sales ratio but instead its ratio of profits to value added, and what matters for the distributive role of profits in a societal context is analogously the economy's aggregate profits-to-value-added ratio. The total share of profit included in the final price of a stereo set is the interesting measure—not just the part of that share going to the company that finally assembles the components and then sells the unit. Not surprisingly, people responding to opinion surveys tend to answer as if they had been asked the important question (What is the economy's profits-to-value-added ratio?) rather than the usual one (What is its profits-to-sales ratio?). Their guesses are still somewhat too high, but even the interpretation of the public's misperceptions is itself subject to contradictions.

The Public Utility Syndrome

The principal contribution of any debate on an issue fundamental to both economics and politics is its implications about what to do next. After as comprehensive an assessment as is possible of the theory and evidence describing the allocative and distributive roles of profits, what should be done?

At least in the United States, sweeping reform or wholesale restructuring of the basics of the economic system seems highly improbable for the foreseeable future. The central planning systems used by many foreign economies, especially Communist countries, offer little attraction as an allocative replacement for the profit system, and it is doubtful that they are compatible with other important social and political values which Western civilization holds along with the generally accepted ideal of greater equality. There also appears to be little popular appetite for direct adoption of classical socialism, and the potential surrogate represented by the steadily growing share of private assets held by pension funds is indeed increasing in importance—but only slowly.

The cutting edge of the debate over the role of profits lies instead at the margin of countless policy issues, each of which individually appears as an issue to resolve within the outlines of the current system, but all of which, taken together over an extended period of time, in fact determine the evolution of the system itself. Although many aspects of this ongoing stream of policy issues are highly relevant to the profits question, the greatest real impact on the role of profits seems most likely to come from the maze of decisions involved in government's increasingly pervasive regulatory structure. The role of government in determining what products business makes, how it produces them, and under what circumstances (and sometimes at what price) it sells them can grow either with or in place of the profit system. Public policy can do its crucial job of preventing harmful externalities like pollution and unsafe products, and promoting beneficial ones like energy independence, either by direct prohibition (thereby obviating the motivating force of profits) or by tax and fee schedules that internalize the externalities (thereby exploiting the profit motive). Despite much discussion of the latter approach—most recently some economists have even suggested a "tax-oriented incomes policy" to encourage businesses to promote price stability by internalizing some of the inflationary consequences of their wage and price decisions—the dominant thread of the growing government interaction with the private sector since World War II has instead followed the regulatory-fiat approach. The government has opted for maximum pollution standards rather than effluent taxes, for example, and for minimum mileage standards rather than either gasoline taxes or a tax-and-subsidy system according to the performance of new cars. The role of profits in allocative decisions can only diminish as the scope and detail of such regulation increase.

Perhaps even more important for the long-run role of profits is the particular nature of the dialogue which has evolved between government and business. When the auto industry opposes safety standards, or the coal industry resists environmental restrictions, or the steel industry seeks tariff protection, or the oil industry defends depletion allowances, the industry's profit position inevitably enters the discussion. Either the industry "needs" a ruling or legislation in its favor because its profits are somehow inadequate, or it can "withstand" an adverse development because its profits are sufficient. In either case, the size of the industry's profits implicitly becomes an object of government policy. The same pattern applies even more explicitly to government's reactions to price and wage increases—with or without formally legislated controls. The steel company president summoned to Washington on Tuesday to defend a sheet-product price increase before a group of government officials is, in principal, free to be as uncompromising as he wishes. But he will probably have to deal with colleagues of the same officials when he returns on Thursday seeking protection from foreign imports, or again on Friday petitioning for an environmental variance to permit construction of a new rolling mill.

The net result of countless such situations through time is that a "public utility syndrome" ultimately replaces a genuine profit system for both allocative and distributive purposes. Even companies in industries not formally subject to rate-of-return regulation deal with government on a basis which presumes that they are somehow entitled to neither more nor less than a "fair return." Shortfalls of profits from the presumed fair return are grounds for government assistance, in any of many available forms, while excesses lead to government opposition. As a result, in the short run the determination of the rate of return in any business becomes even more explicitly a political matter, subject to further domination by the relative power of the various interested constituencies, and market forces play a correspondingly reduced role. Moreover, in a longer time frame, unless the government sets such rates of return at the value implied by the market, the required participation of the government itself can only increase further. If the arbitrarily set rate is too high in some business, investors will want to expand it, and the government will be able to maintain the high rate of return only by forbidding entry or somehow continually widening its support. Alternatively, if the arbitrarily set rate is too low, investors will want to put no further capital into the business, and the government will have to find another means of sustaining it.

Although the "public utility syndrome" is a caricature of government-business interactions in the U.S. economy, it nevertheless contains more than a kernel of truth. More significantly, it rather points toward the direction in which the economy is currently moving than describes where it now stands. If the debate over the role of profits has a practical impact, it will probably be either to accelerate or to retard this motion by respectively emphasizing or demoting the part which informed opinion wants profits to play in individual case-by-case public-policy decisions.

2
The Role of Profits in a Mixed Economy: Changes in the Perceived Reality

Paul A. Samuelson

Profit is today a fighting word. The capitalistic way of life, free private enterprise, its admirers tell us is a system of profit and loss. Profits are the lifeblood of the economic system, the magic elixir upon which progress and all good things ultimately depend.

One man's lifeblood is another man's cancer. In other quarters, profit is simply an exploitative surplus which fat men with an unfair penchant for arithmetic skim off from the gross national product, leaving the worthy true producers of that gross national product with a mere subsistence.

The fireworks of semantics set off by the word *profit* are merely a reflection of the tension and debate going on in every modern mixed economy concerning the proper role of the market-oriented private sector and the state-financed public sector. And it is part of the related perpetual floating debate going on between those who strive for greater egalitarianism both of opportunity and of condition and those who favor the status quo ante bellum, and by *ante bellum* I mean prior to the war over the proper way of taxing pretax income and wealth.

The swing group in these perpetual struggles is composed of those who hanker for less inequality, other things being equal, but who are concerned with the tactical and strategic considerations involved with the deadweight loss that may be incurred in the further pushing of equalizing measures and with what the political traffic will bear in a milieu where the electorate will not always put their money where their rhetoric points.

You will have to forgive me, therefore, if the logical thread of the discussion leads me to stray from the narrow province of profit theory. These will not be digressions or detours but rather necessary explorations of connected territories.

You will also have to forgive me if, as first speaker, I poach on some of the topics in which Professors Arrow and Lundberg have prime property rights. I have an exaggerated respect for the rights of private property, but what would be the advantage of going first if one could not skim off the cream of the discussion in an imperialist fashion?

My self-judged task is to analyze profit from the standpoint of the professional economist. It is proper that I give warning of what is most definitely not going to be my focus on this occasion. This is worth doing because the approach that I am *not* taking is very much the approach that many business people take toward the problem. Let me paint with an impressionistic brush the picture as they see it. Here goes the story.

Once upon a time business enterprise was respected. Calvin Coolidge was accurate when he said that, "the business of America is business," and it was a sad day for all the American people—workers as well as farmers—when Coolidge's statement came to be regarded as a sign of his crudity and of his having sold out to plutocracy.

Today it is another story. Profit *is a dirty word.* Business *is a dirty word.* Businessman *is a dirty word. The public is woefully uninformed on what fraction of the dollar spent goes to profit. What has happened to our educational system that students do not learn in high school and in college economics courses that only a few pennies of each sale dollar go to profits? And why don't our college professors get across the message that even those few pennies left over after heavy taxation do not go simply to finance the riotous and unnecessary consumption expenditures of a few wealthy families, but rather that it is out of those pennies of profits that plowed-back earnings will finance the capital formation we so desperately now need? The high real wages of tomorrow will materialize only if the needed increments to capital take place—just as the present-day highest standard of living in the world is enjoyed by the American working person only because the fruits of past thrift have filtered down to him in higher productivity and real wages.*

This being the truth about profits and business—the economic facts of life—what business needs is to get its story across. Although businessmen, as doers, are often at a disadvantage with the glib intellectuals, they must learn to go out on the public platform. They must testify before congressional committees. They must take out full-page ads that educate readers on the function of profits. They must encourage proper economics courses and teaching at the school, college, and inplant-course level. And, within the limits of their powers and influence, businessmen should seek to discourage the dissemination of falsely critical alternative doctrines.

The picture I have painted is a bit of caricature, as brevity makes more or less inevitable. But a no less devastating caricature could be made of the typical position of the antagonists toward business. If I were to read to you short selective passages from *Monopoly Capitalism*, the view of profits given by two eminent American Marxian scholars, Paul Baran and Paul Sweezy, the impression could be given that the cancerous surplus now swallows up much of the United States GNP, and that final disaster is kept at bay only by virtue of cold-war expenditures and imperialism, and by ever more frantic advertising expenditures and other conspicuous wastes.

Mine is not the task of analyzing ideologies, or of sifting out the correct and incorrect hypotheses concerning the real economic world that implicitly lie behind the various articulations of ideology that focus around the topic of profit. Mine is the more prosaic task of looking at what is happening in the last half of the twentieth century to profit and to the general share of the national income that goes to property—looking at all this, I remind you, from the standpoint of the professional economist—to try to understand the process and, perhaps from this understanding, to achieve some feel for the probabilities about future economic developments.

Here is a preview of some hard problems that analysis hopes, in the end, to grapple with:

Has the trend for the rate of profit been downward in the last decade or so in the United States? Has there not been a similar trend discernible for Western Germany and Sweden, for France and Japan, for Italy and Britain, and for the nonsocialist world generally?

If this downward trend can be verified, what are its principal causes? Is it, as many businessmen believe, due primarily to the rapacious demands of the trade unions? Some left wing writers—I think of two from Oxford—essentially agree that profits are down because militant wage bargaining has transferred them to the workers. Unlike the complaining businessmen, however, they look upon this process with favor rather than disfavor. Are either of these groups right in their diagnoses?

Aside from the exactions from profit by plundering labor, it has been argued that governmental regulations serve as a burden on capital's earning power. Control of pollution and agitation by environmentalists undercut the margin of profitability. The extra costs of achieving the last degree of atmospheric and water purity come right off the top of profits. An Alaskan pipeline budgeted to cost $700 million ends up in such a political regime costing $5 billion to $10 billion. A substantial fraction of all the funds available for new gross capital formation is preempted from going into capacity expansion and commercial productivity improvement because it must be siphoned into meeting safety and environmental standards imposed by government and public opinion. No wonder, according to this view, that the profit rate is down.

Or is an alternative explanation valid, one which posits that since World War II there has been a great accumulation of new capital all over the Western world? Capital competes with capital, and in this view it is the competitive "deepening" of capital that explains the putative decline in profit rates.

Keynes, in his now classic 1936 *General Theory*, spoke speculatively about the "euthanasia of the rentier." For this lecture's purposes, this can be translated to mean that capital accumulates enough to bring its return essentially down to zero or close to that level. Can the mixed economy survive, can the capitalist sheep perform their vital function when so little of the wool they grow is left to them?

Obviously, a model that alleges a worldwide decline in the profitability of capital incident to a vast deepening of accumulated capital is a bit at variance with the loud talk we have been hearing of "capital shortage." The president of the stock exchange has calculated with his Hewlett-Packard computer that our capital needs over the next several years are prodigious. Secretary of the Treasury William Simon, a seasoned veteran of Wall Street, points to the new capital needs created by the fivefold increase in OPEC energy prices. George Terborgh and other shrewd observers of current economic history voice concern that fictitious paper profits generated by inflation conceal the true drop in real profit returns and in real corporate savings in the 1970s. The United States has for decades been devoting a smaller fraction of GNP to gross capital formation than have West Germany and Japan; U.S. investment ratio has been smaller even than that of France, Italy, the Netherlands, or Scandinavia. More than a dozen years ago, Simon Kuznets, in one of his classic National Bureau of Economic Research quantitative monographs, put forth the hypothesis that this under-saving by America might well be the result of overspending by the American government. Treating public expenditure as the collective counterpart of private-consumption expenditure, one might argue that it was because the affluent United States was already consuming so much in the pre-Kennedy-Johnson-Nixon years that it was able to invest so little. This raises the question of how to reconcile an implied dearth of capital with low rather than high pretax real returns, and how to explain the puzzle of stagnating real values of equities in a decade of inflation when their reproduction costs have been soaring.

Textbook Treatment of Profit

If you are assigned a topic and have no good ideas on it, your first refuge as an intellectual scoundrel is to go to the dictionary and pluck out a definition of the subject. A second way of marking time before buckling down to hard thought is to turn to an elementary economics textbook for its definitions and classifications. With your indulgence, let me summarize what Chapter 31 of my *Economics* says about profits. Its first sentence says: "In addition to wages, interest, and rent, economics often talks about a fourth category of income: profit." I believe this follows in the tradition of Adam Smith, and on this 200th anniversary of Smith's *The Wealth of Nations*, it is mandatory for a lecturer to bring in the doctrines of that exalted founder of economics.

Smith, like Ricardo and other classical economists, thought it one function of economics to describe and explain the *distribution* of the national income. Smith, however, unlike David Ricardo, did not regard the question of how the social pie is to be divided as the prime and fundamental question of political economy. He was interested as well in the conditions conducive to *growth of the size of the total pie*. We already have here an explicit formulation of a dialectical debate that rages unresolved 200 years later. Conservative writers—Vilfredo Pareto will serve as a good example—urge the public to concentrate on *increasing the total* of national product, resting assured that the different classes of society are likely to share in any increment of the total. Radical critics of the bourgeois order take the opposite tack and insist upon the opposition of interests of the different classes, so that what one class can hope to gain in fractional share of total income must come out of the fractional share of another class.

Just as Adam Smith would break down national income into the wages of labor, the rent of land, the interest on reproducible capital, and a fourth category of entrepreneurial profit, so too did Adam Smith regard the price of any competitive product as being the sum of four necessary components.

First is wage cost to compensate for the *sweat and disutility of human labor.*

Second is interest cost to compensate for what Nassau Senior would 50 years later declare to be *the psychic sweat of the human abstinence and waiting involved in the act of saving for the future rather than consuming now.* Ferdinand LaSalle, the great rival of Karl Marx in the German socialist movement, had a good deal of fun in rhapsodizing about the Herculean sweat of Baron Rothschild in saving his millions of pounds. Still, in terms of apologetics for the different elements of cost and class sharing of income, Smith's first two components are understandable.

When it came to the third component, land rent, David Hume, Adam Smith, David Ricardo, and the American Henry George parted company with the pre-Revolution French Physiocrats who had glorified argiculture as the only productive industry and land as the only producer of true net product. People like to quote Adam Smith to show that he was not a stuffy reactionary. With respect to land owners, Smith pointed out that they love to reap where other men have sown. Land is productive, but not its owners, who are providing no true or honorary sweat deserving of a return. From this follows the notion that true rent—the return to the inexhaustible, nonaugmentable Ricardian land that is the gift of nature—is a most suitable object of taxation, both from an ethical viewpoint and from the viewpoint of involving the least efficiency distortion.

This concept of land rent as an unnecessary surplus is worth keeping in mind. Bernard Shaw and other Fabians later generalized this Ricardo-George doctrine to *all property*, alleging that their return is an unnecessary surplus that can largely be taxed away without production or other nondistributive consequences.

In our own day, an independent mind like Joan Robinson becomes a bit impatient with the idea that the interest and profit return to capital is something "deserved": whatever it took to bring the vector of heterogeneous capital goods into existence, now that they are in existence there is no real reason why the fruits of their combined collaboration with labor should not go almost wholly to labor. Indeed, one can specify technological models in which, if the laboring class as a collusive group militantly insist upon a high real wage that takes most of the total social pie, the resulting low level of profit involves no great penalties in terms of maintenance of production. Mrs. Robinson, and other members of the Cambridge-Italian neo-Keynesian school, may agree that the rate of saving and long-term growth of the system may be less if the more thrifty capitalists have their incomes decimated; but even this could be overcome by having the state do the saving conducive to more rapid growth.

Austrian economists less radical than Robinson—I have Böhm-Bawerk, Gottfried Haberler, and Lionel Robbins in mind—like to dispense with psychic disutility in favor of "opportunity-cost" theories of price determination. For such Austrians, the inelasticity of supply of all the factors, nonland as well as land, means that their rents can be taxed without distorting substitution effects and deadweight loss. They differ from Robinson in that they regard the returns to property as being well determined by economic laws independently of power bargaining—as if, so to speak, by a vast Cobb-Douglas, J.B. Clark Austrian production function for aggregate output. But in terms of policy, their model lends itself to agreement with her conclusion, in that redistributive taxation by the state could, in effect, make workers the owners of the nonhuman factors of production, or at least of their fruits.

Those who call themselves socialists fall into at least two groups: Marxists and the others. Modern economists like Abba Lerner, James Meade, and Oskar Lange (before he went back to Poland after World War II) have tended to become impatient with the vulgar Marxian notion that the labor theory of value has some factual or scientific validity. To insist that labor is the sole source of value in a system where labor, land, natural resources, and various productive inputs that have been manufactured in the past are allocated in a time-phased way to produce streams of different kinds of outputs, consumer goods, and intermediate outputs—this they regard as *unuseful*. All that is required according to egalitarians of this non-Marxian viewpoint is to say:

Nonhuman inputs are productive in creating outputs along with human inputs. But the technical indispensability of those nonhuman factors has nothing to do with the indispensability of their owners. Their owners are quite dispensable. They can be dispossessed of their ownership by capital levies, by expropriation without compensation, by expropriation with full or partial compensation, or by redistributive taxation of the incomes they derive from property.

It is true that people like Abba Lerner have been saying this for more than 40 years without being particularly listened to by the Marxists or, for that matter, by the propertied interests and electoral majorities. But not being listened to is a fate they share with Marxians and with numerous other critics of the existing mixed-economy order.

I began to list Adam Smith's four components of price and of national income. Before getting to the fourth I digressed into the views of later writers. Most of my discussion about the fractional returns to property and labor, as those shares work themselves out in the marketplace or as they are altered by governmental policies, could be carried on without ever even mentioning the word *profit*. Indeed, the words *interest* or *capital yield* could for the most part do the work of the word *profit*. And on the whole, Smith does work with a three-sector model of wages, rent, and interest.

But if memory serves, Adam Smith did sometimes make the further distinction between profit and interest. Thus, in the informed-man-of-the-world fashion that characterizes Smith's writings, he somewhere speaks of the rate of interest as being 6 percent at the same time the rate of profit is 12 percent. How neat that one is just double the other, but no neater than the convenient fiction of pre-Smith and post-Smith writers that national revenue, like an estate revenue, is split up into even thirds: one-third for the worker, one-third for the operator or employer, and one-third for the land owner.

When an eighteenth century writer put the rate of profit above the rate of interest, what did he have in mind? First, he usually had in mind *the differential return to some kind of management:* extra effort by the entrepreneur in handling funds and making productive decisions—and perhaps extra cleverness on his part in so doing. Today we would tend to call this the wages—high wages to be sure—of responsible managers. Because they make decisions so important for huge sums of money, the wages they command are high. Because they handle such large sums, Smith thought it made good sense to pay them well lest they abuse their trust or handle it carelessly. Because great talent in doing these important things is rare, the wage rents that are earned by those with such scarce genetic and educational advantages are handsome. A modern intermediate writer would treat these differentials completely as wages rather than profits, except for the realistic possibility that it may be optimal to give such high-talented workers a profit-sharing interest in the fortunes of the concern. This makes it something of a hybrid, poised between wages and interest or profit.

There is a second notion that early writers had in mind when speaking of a profit premium over and above the safe rate of interest. The capitalist owner of an enterprise was regarded as the risk taker of last resort. He paid out wages and rent; he paid out interest on capital borrowed from a passive rentier group; he produced with these acquired inputs; and he bought merchandise for sale. However, the ability to sell goods at satisfactory price is never assured in advance. One ship venture may be very profitable; but positive profit premium over and above the interest rate might well be cancelled off in the next venture which would be unsuccessful.

From the point of view of *profit as the chance algebraic premium above and below the interest rate*, one might on the average find no positive profit share and no positive average differential of profit over and above the interest rate. However, for that to be the case, risks in the long run would have to be fairly predictable even though chancy in the short run. And furthermore, capitalists would have to be fairly neutral with respect to risk taking, ready to accept a ducat if the fair coin turns up heads and lose a ducat if the coin turns up tails. However, suppose it is more realistic to assume that just as it is a human propensity to wish to shun the disutility of work and to shun giving up consumption today in favor of consumption tomorrow, so it is a human propensity to wish to shun the disutility and sweat of risk taking. In that case, those industries which are subject to heavy irreducible risks would in the long run find that their goods would be priced so as to cover not only the wage of labor, the rent of land, and the interest rate of needed capital, but also the positive risk or insurance premium needed to cover the disutility of risk taking. By means of reinsurance and hedging in speculative markets, the irreducible risks might be cut down and shifted more evenly over the community; but to the extent that an irreducible residuum of riskiness remains, a Smithian would expect price to include some compensation for it. Similarly, some component of the GNP, hard as it might be to identify and measure, would be the *profit return to risk taking.*

Chapter 31 of the elementary textbook had to point out that the current statistics on profits put out by the Department of Commerce by no means measure this fourth concept of profit. Corporation profits plus earnings of nonincorporated enterprise are a catchall of *implicit interest return* on capital provided by the owners of the businesses—in the case of smaller business, of *implicit wage earnings* of the proprietors, farmers, and professional people. There may be *some component of risk premium,* but how large it is or even what its algebraic sign is, there is no way of inferring from the figures themselves.

That chapter also had to point out several difficulties with the Smith and post-Smith concepts of profits:

1. Frank Knight has questioned whether people are risk averse, arguing that often they embrace risk without compensation or even pay for the privilege. Although he could be right, the bulk of the stock market evidence on the tradeoff between risk and return suggests that people as a whole do act as if they are risk averse. But Knight's skepticism goes on to argue that most uncertainties in real life are not at all amenable to the mathematical probabilities of risk. Thus, when the National Bureau reports that a person would have done better buying second-class bonds from 1920 to 1950 than buying gilt-edge highest-quality bonds, a Knightian would reply: "History is a one-time story. If the United States had not come out of the Great Depression as it did—and that was a perfectly possible outcome on which mathematical odds cannot be defined—gilt-edge bonds would have done better." So most of pure profit might be regarded as simply the discrepancy in an uncertain world between what people thought might happen and what actually happens.

2. Schumpeter put great stress in his theory of profit on the unforeseeable gains the innovator can temporarily get before imitators come in to compete away his necessarily temporary surplus returns.

3. Adam Smith was for the most part thinking of the interest and profit earnings of reasonably competitive enterprises. In a Galbraithian view of the world, most of the large corporations do not live in the dream world of effective competition. I do not know what Galbraith's theory of the share of profits is: his last books have not told us why they are as large as they are, and why they are not larger. The late Michael Kalecki of Poland attempted to create a theory of the profit share based on an alleged constancy of "the degree of market imperfection." But even when one reformulates his model to make it applicable to the real world, it is dangerously like one of those theories which the logicians can reduce to the tautology "Things are what they are because that is what they are." One does not get excited by the remark that morphine puts us to sleep by virtue of its soporific quality, but that bored reaction should not blind us to the fact that morphine does put one to sleep. As I have tried to understand the trends in the distribution of income, remarks about the degree of deviation of actual market conditions from the competitive model have not seemed to have predictive or explanatory content.

4. Time limitations require me to be dogmatically brief concerning proposed macroeconomic theories of income distribution. Nicholas Kaldor in 1955 floated the theory that spontaneous changes in investment spending, instead of producing changes in money and real GNP, in fact have no effects in moving a system from its full-employment position: the only effect of the changes in the investment multiplicand is to change the share of profits enough to bring full-employment saving into equality with the new level of investment. Kaldor has been called "Jean Baptiste Kaldor" for this full-employment model. However, events of the 20 years since its creation have not given us full employment or evidence confirming the model. The more cautious long-run theories of Robinson and Pasinetti have been of little explanatory value in interpreting what seem to have been the facts about profits in the last two decades.

Marxian Paradigms for Profit

Having quoted mainstream economists from Adam Smith to post-Keynesian writers, I must be ecumenical and take note of Marxian formulations. The law of the declining rate of profit is one tenet of such analysis. Karl Marx hoped to lay bare the laws of motion of developing capitalism by means of his novel analysis of surplus value.

The broad historical facts of the last century have involved a rising trend in real wages, a fractional share of wages in national income that is either constant or gently rising, and long-term meandering of the real rate of profit or interest.

A basic Marxian model that postulates a definable reproduction cost for wage labor is capable of defining a determinable rate of steady-state profit provided all goods are producible by time-phased labor and themselves as inputs.

The resulting steady-rate rate of profit will be constant in the absence of technical change. The level of this equilibrium interest or profit rate is definable without any recourse to Marx's novel algorithm in which the rate of surplus-value markup is reckoned on direct labor costs alone and is uniform between industries. The methods of Sraffa, Leontief, and other modern analysts benefit in no degree from Marx's novelties of analysis. But even if one waives this controversial point, the predictive implications of postulating a reproduction cost for labor at a meaningful, conventional subsistence level would be incompatible with the actual historical facts of a meandering profit rate and rising real wage rates. Logically, the paradigm should have implied a rising rate of profit from 1867 to 1976, a stagnant pattern for real wages, and a falling fractional labor share in the national income. (To grapple with the damnable difficulties of understanding and predicting real-world complexities, one will accept help from any source, however unpopular it might be with the conservative interests of plutocracy. Alas, perusal of the analyses proferred by Marxists abroad or at home has not deemed to reward analysts of the past, present, and future.)

Falling Profit, a Normal Thing?

If the expert jury does conclude that the profit rate has been falling worldwide this decade, that would not be a finding abhorrent or even surprising to Adam Smith and David Ricardo. Like Karl Marx, Smith and Ricardo each predicted the profit rate would fall. While the system was growing through accumulation, the fall in profit rate, Smith thought, would temporarily raise the real wage rate above the reproduction cost of labor. The fact of population growth itself, Smith thought, was a sign of wage prosperity. Ricardo saw perhaps more clearly than Smith that growth could not continue in a balanced exponential mode forever. The scarcity of land would invoke the law of diminishing returns. Since labor would always emerge from the fertile womb in the abundance needed to bring the real wage down to labor's cost of reproduction, Ricardo deduced that capital accumulation would reduce the interest rate to a minimum, and that a lower profit rate and an unchanged real wage rate had to imply that land rent collectors were the ultimate beneficiaries of progress.

By 1912 Schumpeter's classic *Economic Development* argued in a similar fashion for a decline in the rate of interest and profit to zero. By 1912 the human womb was no longer so fertile. Hence Schumpeter expected that both labor owners and land owners would reap the benefit of the capital deepening. At least this was Schumpeter's schemata in the absence of innovation and technical change. Why were Smith, Ricardo, and Schumpeter so comfortable with the prospect of virtual euthanasia of the interest-receiving classes? Remember that all three were essentially believers in Say's law, according to which there could never be underspending and involuntary unemployment.

Malthus, Sismondi, Hobson, Keynes, and most nonacademic economists were not so confident that there is a law of conservation of purchasing power which rules out unemployment and excessive hoarded savings. Marx believed that capitalists would be stimulated by any incipient drop in the profit rate to initiate labor-saving inventions to hold down real wages. He perhaps did not sufficiently realize that this would be likely to negate his law of the declining rate of profit. Rosa Luxemburg, Lenin, and other post-Marxian analysts of imperialism held that advanced capitalistic countries would need desperately to rely on colonies and exploitive foreign investment to put off the evil day of euthanasia and mass unemployment.

Innovation versus Diminishing Returns

It is almost exactly 40 years ago that Keynes's *General Theory* set off the Keynesian revolution. The universe of economics has not been the same since. Let me sum up the outlook for the rate of profit just prior to that bombshell. Schumpeter, Irving Fisher, Cannan, Pigou, and Hicks all agreed with the Smith-Ricardo march toward low profit rates to the drumbeat of capital accumulation and deepening. But as an offset to movements down static curves of diminishing returns, they all envisaged a quasi-random chain of invention and technical change. They expected the result to be a more or less endless Brownian vibration of the profit rate at average levels determined by the pace and character of invention relative to the rapidity of capital accumulation. Their model seemed to provide an appropriate fit to the stylized facts of capitalistic development: rising real wage rates, relatively constant factor shares, and meandering rates of profit.

Joan Robinson has taught us to recognize that this simplified parable of neoclassical economics is overly simple. My colleague, Robert Merton, working in a tradition first explored by Oxford's James Mirrlees, has shown how a one-sector, one-capital-good model subject to white-noise, Harrod-neutral technical change can be given an exact formulation. For it, the real wage does rise on the average; the real rate of profit does display a Brownian wobble according to an ergodic probability distribution; and depending on how closely the oscillating production function approximates the elasticity substitution of unity, the resulting factor shares tend to change little over time.

Mrs. Robinson regards such a flexible "leets" model as hopelessly unrealistic (*leets* is *steel* spelled backward, an inside joke). Such a model evades the problem of limitations on technical substitutability. It evades the problem of how to reduce a changing vector of heterogeneous capital goods to some scalar quantum measure of platonic capital. It evades what is called the "Hahn problem," which more than a decade ago Frank Hahn posed in the following form.

Given multivarious demands and capital goods, how does an unplanned market system know what path of productions and prices to aim for and follow?

There are an infinite number of alternative paths it could follow this next year with apparent equality of yield in every industry. Yet, as Hahn and other writers have suggested, only one of the infinity of paths can be a *permanent* equilibrium path, self-warranted by its own fulfillment. In the absence of omniscient planning or of a utopian system of perfect futures markets quoting prices on everything from now 'til Kingdom Come, how does a mixed economy organize itself with even a tolerable approximation to effective performance?

Writeoffs on REIT loans and urban condominiums provide examples that the Hahn problem is a genuine one. The wonder is that the examples are not more numerous. Most of the time, it is the macroeconomic malfunctioning of the system—inflations, slumps, and stagnations—that occasions greatest concern. Only intermittently do microeconomic malfunctionings force their way to the top of the agenda for economists' concern.

One understands the real world the best one can. Often that "best" is unsatisfactorily good. One may pragmatically evade the Hahn perplexity by conceiving of the real world as a generalized Merton-Solow model of many industries and alternative processes involving congeries of heterogeneous inputs. As tastes and technology change in ways only partially predictable, the system, so to speak, keeps re-aiming its motions toward configurations that are more or less self-warranting and maintainable, avoiding Ponzi-like tulip manias and necessarily transient changes in the terms of trade between various goods.

This admittedly fuzzy and less-than-satisfactory model, looked at from the perpsective of the longer-run economic historian, may be hypothesized to have some of the general properties of the oversimple Solow-Merton "leets" model:

It displays rising real wage rates from technical change. It displays meandering average profit rates over a decade depending on whether the life-cycle accumulation of capital is checked fully or partly by labor-saving or capital-saving technical change. The relative share of labor (inclusive of the return to "human capital" in the form of past investments into education and training) need not change systematically much in one direction or the other relative to the share of property (inclusive of rents from land, interest, dividends, and imputed accounts to equity ownership).

There is no logical necessity that the real world actually behaves much like this fuzzy paradigm. But as the Nobel biologist Peter Medawar reminds us, serious scientists struggle with the *tractable*: and until a better wheel comes to town, serious players at the game of understanding developments in the modern mixed economy will have to use the best wheel available. Some young economist in the room may win a Nobel Prize for devising such a better wheel—and I wish her Godspeed on the task!

Rectifying Investment Distortion

Taking a Toynbean world view—and no lesser viewpoint is relevant—I do *not* on balance discern a dearth of capital, except in the trivial sense that having more of all producible inputs would bring per capita consumption potential nearer to the maximal golden-rule state. If fewer of us wasted time, if the first seven laws of thermodynamics could be repealed, if, other things being equal, one had more capital goods—it is an uninteresting truism that productivity would be enhanced. And if my Aunt Sally had wheels, she'd be a stage coach.

There is a less trivial sense in which "capital shortage" is worth investigating. Any income tax system like the American one puts a wedge between the pretax return to society of having more capital and the posttax return to the investor deciding whether to trade off some current consumption goods against some future consumption goods. In addition, as Martin Feldstein has been analyzing, modern systems of state-financed old-age pensions may inhibit the level of capital formation in comparison with what the people would choose to save and invest in a private system that is kept running at full employment by central-bank policies that ensure no aborting of thrift in stagnation.

A case can therefore be made along lines argued decades ago by Myrdal, Tobin, me, and others of "socialization of thrift" in the following sense:

The central bank keeps real interest rates low enough to induce real capital formation at a pace sufficient to offset the extra savings generated by tight fiscal policies dictated by an enlightened electorate.

Attractive as this possibility might seem to be, in actual life, Burns, Wallich, and their fellow governors of the Federal Reserve System find themselves acting out the role of inflation fighters of last resort: fiscal ease voted by the people is used to offset monetary tightness contrived by the Central Bank. I blame no one for this Greek comedy—or perhaps tragedy—but must point out that the scenario is a reversal of the Myrdal-Tobin-Samuelson script.

Capital "Glut"?

Having made the preceding concessions to the notion of a possible capital shortage, I must state that the bulk of the evidence points in the opposite direction. As I survey the many studies made on real profit yields, the story seems to be thus: in Western Europe or North America, in Japan or Australasia, real earning rates of capital show a declining trend during the last decade or two. The decline is more acute in Italy and Britain than in the United States and Germany. But qualitatively the pattern is similar everywhere.

The study by William Nordhaus of Yale, in the 1974 *Brookings Papers on Economic Activity*, provides an excellent example. After correction for aberrations of inflation accounting, both before and after taxes there is a steady downdrift of the real profit rate. A dozen similar studies for Sweden, West Germany, Britain, and elsewhere tell the same story.

My MIT colleague Fischer Black reminds me how difficult it is to detect a genuine trend in the real return on capital. To know it, you must have a firm measure of capital's value at the beginning and end of the period. Since stock market valuations are so much like a random walk—a tale about white noise told by 30 million idiots and prudent men—the proper corrections to historic book values are hard to come by. Still there must be some pattern of evidence suggestive of stationary or declining real yields even for a Wiener-Itô-Merton stochastic diffusion process. And my Bayesian probabilities make me inclined to bet that the 1960-1974 trend, if not the 1950-1976 trend, has been somewhat downward.

Nordhaus provides an explanatory hypothesis for the fall of the profit rate. Perhaps, he speculates, it has fallen because risk-averse investors regard profits as less chancy than they used to be. On reflection, I am inclined to doubt this explanation. Investors have never seemed so jumpy and unsure of themselves as in the 1965-1975 decade. The failure of the stock market to serve as a hedge against inflation in this last decade has induced in the bourgeoisie a failure of nerve hardly consonant with the Nordhaus explanation.

From Glut to Dearth?

Capital glut rather than capital shortage provides a better scientific fit to the actual facts. But of course capital glut at one time can induce capital shortage at another. Perhaps the surprising strengths in real profit rates in 1975-1976 are the first signs that an element of capital shortage is beginning to be generated by the very stagnation of the Nixon-Ford 1970s epoch.

Those would be the signs a scientist would look for. Rather than agreeing with the fashionable postulate that an increased degree of oligopoly power explains the surprising improvement in profitability, one might keep a watchful eye out for the possibility that the OPEC energy crisis and the recession shortfalls in fixed investment are beginning to induce a rise in competitive capital yields.

However, given the facts on excess capacities in many different lines, it would be premature to declare the demise of capital glut and the arrival of capital shortage.

Puzzle of Falling Equity Values

A 10-hour speech could not do justice to the basic problems posed in these Diebold lectures. Only a few words can be spared to discuss the paradox of a stagnant stock market over a decade of inflation.

Perhaps the 1975-1976 rise will blow away the paradox. But even with the Dow Jones Industrial Index back once again to 1000, the following oddity requires explanation:

A decade ago the equity averages were about the same as today. Thus you can buy the earning assets of the U.S. economy for not very much more money than it would have cost 10 years ago. (I exaggerate a bit, since one must correct for new debt and make other adjustments.) Yet in the last 10 years, the cost of living, labor, and raw materials have all risen steadily and irreversibly. If you were to buy those same earning assets (plant, equipment, inventories, intangibles) in the commodity markets—at their production costs (or reproduction costs after depreciation adjustments)—you would find the total price has soared in comparison with 10 years ago.

All this has been nicely documented by estimates of Tobin and Bischoff at Yale. How do we explain this paradoxical discrepancy?

1. An important possibility is that equities were grossly overvalued in 1965. Newton's law of action and reaction then accounts for part of the discrepancy.

2. A second argument is fashionable but partially misleading. When a system goes from a low 1965 inflation rate to a higher equilibrium rate of 1975 inflation, nominal interest rates gradually adjust upward. So to speak, the price/earnings (p/e) multiple of bonds is lower at higher anticipated inflation rates. The argument goes on to assert: "Since common stocks must compete with bonds for the investors' favor, a drop in the equilibrium price/earnings price multiple of bonds must dictate a corresponding drop in price/earnings multiple of common stocks. So the post-1965 drop in real value of common stocks, far from being paradoxical, actually represents the needed once-and-for-all adjustment to a new equilibrium rate of inflation."

There is some grain of truth in this argument. But inflation-induced distortions in real tax rates aside, careful analysis can show cogent models in which the price/earnings multiple of common stocks should be the same at a high rate of anticipated inflation as at a low rate once all transient adjustments have taken place. (I do not wish to pronounce here on the merits or demerits of the view of John Lintner and others that, when inflation first accelerates and *while* the system is adjusting to a new higher permanent rate of inflation, the p/e ratios of stocks will systematically (and even rationally) fall. My colleague at MIT, Fischer Black, doubts this. Only an extended analysis could narrow down and appraise the disagreements.)

3. A third explanation offered for stagnation of stock prices has nothing essentially to do with inflation. Stipulating a deepening of capital which lowers the interest or profit yield on capital, shouldn't we expect this to show itself in a decline of rentier earnings and common stock prices? The economic theorists can by no means agree in giving necessarily affirmative answers to these separable questions.

First, the increase in the total of capital might be greater in percentage terms than the drop in the yield in each unit of capital. Thus *total* capitalists' yield might rise rather than fall. To be sure, this would be little comfort to your great aunt living off an unenlarged quantum of capital. To the person looking at his shares of a corporation that has been paying out its earnings in dividends and preserving the same size of operations, the size of those dividends per share would admittedly go down. But that is to say no more than that the yield on capital, expressed as an interest rate or profit rate, has gone down in accordance with the stipulated hypothesis.

Although a deepening of capital might result in no fall in its absolute total yield, even an unchanged absolute total could become a declining fractional share of the growing total of real national income. So the propertied classes might lose relative position.

Worse than that, it may be realistic to expect that the overall elasticity of substitution between capital goods and human labor is low enough so that property's absolute share is made to decline by the deepening of capital. Part of the malaise of the upper-middle-income and upper classes might result from this possibility.

Suppose for the sake of the argument that it is. Does that explain the fall in the real value of a typical common stock? The theorist must point out that a drop in interest rates is definitely not the same thing as a drop in the capitalized value of the earnings of a property. A postulated halving of the rate of interest, say from 10 down to 5 percent, would double the price/earnings multiple of a dollar of perpetual earning stream. It is a merit of the oversimplified Solow one-sector "leets" model that in it, a deepening of capital which lowers the profit rate unmistakeably has absolutely no effect on the value of a unit of old capital expressed in terms of a market basket of consumption goods.

We are still left, then, with a puzzle over explanation of the stagnating real values of all equities. It is not beyond the ingenuity of the economic theorist to dream up some pattern of capital-saving innovation which would destroy forever much of the value of existent capital goods. These dreary days it is hard for a physician to distinguish between paranoia and rational concern. Still, I would have to regard it as premature to put much credence in a scenario alleging dire outlook for incomes from property.

Conclusion and Outlook

An old hand at college lecturing learns to pace himself so that the end of the classroom hour arrives just as he has brought the discussion to the springboard between the past and the future. The present is that part of the past which has the greatest relevance for the future.

Moses-like, I have been leading you chosen people through the wilderness of the economic present. Like Moses, it is not given to me to enter omnisciently into the promised future. I must leave to Joshua—I mean to Professors Arrow and Lundberg—the triumph of resolving the uncertainties of the future, responding successfully to the title of these third John Diebold lectures, "New Challenges to the Role of Profit." As an economic theorist, I will venture only the following speculation about the promised land of the last quarter of the twentieth century.

I suspect that economic historians will judge the third quarter of the twentieth century to have been a vintage epoch for the mixed economy. Every year in Bordeaux is not a vintage year. Regression toward the mean is as real in economics as it is in biology. Though one expects the economic order to end neither in a bang nor a whimper, it would be rash of me to project for the quarter century ahead the sprint of economic growth of the quarter century behind us. Therein I suspect lies the true challenge to the role of profit, rather than from trade union headquarters, national capitals, or campfires of the Sierra Club.

Commentary

Eli Shapiro

As Professor Samuelson so ably points out, challenges to profits are all around us
in all the world's economies and have been with us through the nineteenth and
twentieth centuries, at least. In the 1930s in the United States and elsewhere,
there was concern over the plight of the poorest one-third and over the pricing
behavior and profit position of business and its "trusts." While certain social
critics sound the same concerns at the moment, something new has been added
to the struggle over profits. This something new is a better articulated statement
by business that capital investment requires a reasonable expectation of returns
in order to attract the necessary savings, and that these necessary returns must
be generated by appropriate pricing of products in markets. There are several
reasons for this campaign on the part of business. One is that business feels it
was drawn off course by the behavior of profits over the past 10 years. Looked
at after the fact, many investment projects have turned out to be much less
profitable than initially expected. In addition, the enormous investment requirements that seem to be warranted by the changing relative price of energy or raw
materials lead business to be quite concerned as to whether product prices will
be allowed to stay high enough for a long enough time to justify the investments
it undertakes. Finally, many firms are concerned about their ability to charge
high enough prices to generate profits on their existing investments in light of
their past investment experience and the uncertain future.

Professor Samuelson's paper makes clear the two different roles which
profits play in any economy. First, capital is a scarce resource, and its use must
be rationed. Goods, whose production requires capital, must be priced high
enough to reflect this use of a scarce resource, and profits reflect the price that
must be charged for capital. Efficient operation of either a socialist or a private
economy requires this role for profits. Second, paying profits to the individual
suppliers of capital can be the device for inducing society to abstain from
current consumption in return for the prospect of greater future consumption.
To the extent that this incentive system gives rise to perceived income
inequalities, however, there is pressure to separate the roles of profits as an
element of costs and prices from profits as an element of the income
distribution. Samuelson states that the impact of private profits on the
distribution of income is a central source of the friction over profits. He further
states that society has to deal with the problem as a tradeoff between the
objectives of equity and efficiency.

He goes on to argue that it is possible to keep profits as an element of costs
and prices but not have profits as an element of income. One could use the tax
system to capture profit income and to determine the total of saving and a

collective distribution of debt and equity funds to determine the allocation of this saving to investment. He points out that such a social system might reduce incentives to take risk or to exert effort, and that it might involve misjudgments and, by reducing efficiency, reduce the growth in real output. As he puts it, there is a tradeoff between equity and efficiency as society moves to deal with the income-distribution effects of treating profits as a return to private capital.

I agree that there is such a tradeoff, and that Professor Samuelson has stated it well. I hasten to add that he has not taken a position on how this tradeoff should be resolved. Having said that, and recognizing that personal choices are subjective, I shall take advantage of my role as discussant to say that it is my view that the correct resolution lies in fostering efficiency and growth. This means that while we do, indeed, have the option to separate profits from income, to do so would in my view cost us more in social well-being than we would gain.

In my view, the poorest third, or whatever is the subject of social and economic policy, will be absolutely better off with their current, possibly inequitable share of the larger pie; that is, the greater growth which would be associated with private profit is likely to provide a setting which will be more conducive to solving income-distribution problems than would a governmental system for attracting and allocating capital.

Professor Samuelson suggests that the major threat which the mixed economy poses to private profits arises from a concern about the distribution of income. The recent inflation suggests to me, however, that the mixed economy may pose additional threats to profits. These threats arise because the mixed economy seems to have an inflationary bias and because during recent inflation, at least, profits in real terms did not maintain themselves.

Some of the forces causing this have been well documented—a corporate tax policy which overstated corporate income by understating depreciation and did not distinguish between capital gains on assets and income from assets, a public policy which tried for a while to regulate prices, and perhaps, a confusion on the part of corporate executives as to the costs they should have been attempting to include in prices. Another important element was the adverse consequences for productivity and costs that resulted from fluctuations in the economy arising from the failure of stabilization policy. Should these forces continue, profits will continue to be limited and capital formation and growth slowed. Once recognized, these problems can be attacked. One can hope they will not reappear, at least to the same extent.

The inflationary reality of the past few years have had at least two further effects which have reduced the attractiveness of corporate equities as an investment vehicle, however. Inflation has raised the return investors should require from equities or, alternatively, reduced the amount of equity which would be forthcoming at a given, expected rate of profitability. First, asset holders have learned that it is risky to acquire long-term fixed-rate debts and have moved to acquire shorter deposits or debts whose returns have quickly adjusted to actual inflation rates. This has meant that corporations find that their interest costs are more closely tied to actual inflation. To the extent that the prices they charge are kept from responding as rapidly, equity holders suffer in inflation.

Second, the fact that corporations have made large-scale commitments to pay pension benefits in the future has further weakened the role of equities as an effective inflation hedge. Since the bulk of these pension promises is indexed to inflation, much of the corporate income which would be associated with inflation will not be available for equity holders.

In effect, we have built up a structure of claims against corporate income in the hands of creditors, workers, and the federal government which is indexed more or less to inflation. If corporate earnings were correspondingly indexed to inflation, these developments would pose no special threat to equities or requirements for profits. It would, however, mean that equities were no longer the favored inflation hedge. However, to the extent that the prices of corporate products are not allowed the flexibility needed for such a response, or to the extent that stabilization policy causes more fluctuations in productivity, equities would become an inferior inflation hedge and the required rate of return on equities would rise. That is, a critical requirement for the growth of business investment in the mixed economy is corporate pricing flexibility *and* the development of a stabilization policy which avoids major fluctuations in output, productivity and prices.

Therefore, I have argued that we need growth to achieve our objectives for the income position of the "needy" and not an income-transfer program which reduces private profits. In addition, I have argued that we need individual price flexibility and a stable economy in order to achieve the incentives necessary for investment. In a world painfully aware of the limits to its growth, with all the concern about individual prices at the moment and with the deplorable stabilization policies of the past decade, the achievement of these prerequisites may seem impossible and the outlook bleak. On the contrary, I think our current problem may be our great opportunity. The current deep recession leaves the economy with an enormous potential for growth in output, personal incomes, and profits—and the real possibility of a meaningful decline in inflation. Such a combination of events would go a long way toward achieving many of the objectives for income levels, investment, and growth.

Commentary

Peter Temin

One role of profits is to be a signal and guide for investment. Both Paul Samuelson and Eli Shapiro spoke about the necessity for profits to provide this function of guiding investment into the most profitable uses—Samuelson distinguishing it from the income-distribution process of profits and Shapiro choosing between those two roles. I thought I might raise a question as to how necessary that link is and put this necessity to a small test by looking at it from the perspective of the bicentennial.

One chooses the bicentennial for sentimental reasons, of course, but there are also additional reasons to look at the eighteenth century. It was the period of the Industrial Revolution, and one can argue with some success that there was economic growth during that period. In addition, because it is different from the current situation, one gets a bit of perspective on what is happening today.

Let me follow Samuelson's lead in looking both at the views of economists and the views of businessmen, although I have to do this rather differently than he did, given the lapse of time. First, for economists, read Adam Smith, since it is the bicentennial of *The Wealth of Nations* that we are celebrating. Let me show his view through a few quotes to which I will give a brief commentary. Adam Smith said, "The increase of stock, which raises wages, tends to lower profit." In other words, he was very conscious of the fact that profits were returning to capital. Quoting again, "The proportion which the usual market rate of interest ought to bear to the ordinary rate of clear profit, necessarily varies as profit rises or falls. Double interest is in Great Britain reckoned, what the merchants call, a good, moderate, reasonable profit." In other words, while profits are returned to capital, they are more than simply the ordinary return to capital, i.e., more than the rate of interest. Quoting again, "The consideration of his own private profit is the sole motive which determines the owner of any capital to employ it either in agriculture, in manufactures, or in some particular branch of the wholesale or retail trade." In other words, profits are returned to capital, and profits determine the rate of investment, i.e., the allocation of investment into different areas. And then finally, just to complete the argument, "It is the stock that is employed for the sake of profit, which puts into motion the greater part of the useful labor of every society." Investment is not just interesting for its own sake, it is interesting because it leads to employment and production.

Now this view, of course, is not unfamiliar. It is very close to the view of businessmen as reported by Samuelson. It is also the argument behind the famous phrase of the "invisible hand." Samuelson commented on the divergent views of the economists and businessmen today. The question that we might pose is Was there a divergent view between economists (Adam Smith) and businessmen then?

This is hard question to answer because we can't go back and interview businessmen of that era. But we can look at their accounting methods and try to figure or reason from the way they allocated their income where they thought that income came from. In other words, we can look at what they did in their bookkeeping as a clue to how they thought. And as one looks there, one discovers that there was indeed a split then, as there appears to be today between the economist and the businessman.

Before we go into how the accounting was done, we ought to recognize that accounting in the Industrial Revolution was a major intellectual problem. We are talking about accounting for industrial enterprises which used fixed capital and produced goods on the basis of investment. We have to recognize that this was essentially a new activity in the eighteenth century. There had been various forms of economic activity, of course, but they did not fit into this kind of framework. For example, there were accounting systems set up for landed estates, a predominant mode of production. But the purpose of this accounting was not to deal with the results from investments. According to the theory of farming, the land remained year after year and was not changed by investment. The purpose of the accounting was to reduce embezzlement by the steward. The bookkeeping consequently never raised the question of capital: it was set up to measure the income and the outflow.

Alternatively, there was accounting to divide up the profits of merchant adventures. This activity also differs from that of an industrial firm because the firm, if we may call it that, of merchants disbanded after each voyage. There was no problem of continuity. The Fischer Black problem which Samuelson mentioned did not exist at the end of the voyage because you sold everything, wiped out the firm, and divided what was left. You had a clear notion of what was profit. On the other hand, however, you had no sense of what capital was. The question never arose.

The accounting methods for the early industrial firms were adapted from the existing forms of accounting, encompassing various adjustments to the changed circumstances. Most firms were partnerships at the time. The surplus after the payment of expenses and wages was allocated to the partnership, but allocated in two quite separate ways. First of all, interest was given on invested capital. Interest was given at a market rate or at a traditional rate, and then profit was added. So we have the distinction made by Adam Smith: profit was distinct from the ordinary return to capital.

However, the profit, or what was classified as profit, was not allocated according to how much investment people had in the firm. It was allocated according to the original shares in the partnership that made up the firm. These two things could be quite different. They could be different in the beginning because although the share in the partnership might be in return for initial investment, it also might not correspond to an investment. People might take a share in the partnership and then not pay in their investment or be given the share in the partnership for reasons other than their investment. In addition, as time went on, the share in the partnership and the share in the capital stock diverged more and more. Some people reinvested their earnings; other people did not. As a result, there was clear demarcation between an allocation according to the share of invested capital and an allocation according to the share of the partnership. The profits were not allocated in proportion to capital, but rather according to shares in the partnership.

What do we infer from this? What does it imply, this accounting method that we can perceive? First, it implies that businessmen did not see profits, i.e., the income above the rate of interest, as a return to stock, to use Adam Smith's phrase, or to capital, to use our phrase. Another of Adam Smith's points—that profits were returned to stock or returned to capital—was not perceived by eighteenth-century businessmen, as expressed in their accounting technique.

How did the businessmen see profit? Well, as Samuelson has commented, they saw it as a return to entrepreneurship, as a return to risk taking, as a return to individuals and individual behavior, but not as a return to the investment of capital. Consequently, the second implication is that profits did not serve as a guide for investment in the Industrial Revolution. In other words, I argue that this perception affected people's behavior. Profits were seen as not related to investment. When you invested the capital and were given an interest return, it was the same no matter where you invested it. And the question of whether you got profits in addition was related to the structure of the business, to your share in the original agreement, but not to the amount that you invested. Adam Smith's contention that the pursuit of profits determined the composition of investment finds no echo here.

We can conclude that profits played a less important role in the Industrial Revolution than in the traditional story, and that the story of the businessmen implies that they do today or did then. Profits existed. Certainly no one would want to deny that and the certain effects that follow their existence. But in addition to the effects that followed simply from the existence of profits, it has been claimed that there have been effects that followed from the perception of profits. What I would like to suggest here is that this perception may have differed in the eighteenth century from what it is today, and that while this altered perception may or may not have functioned as a difficulty in industrial growth, it was hardly a barrier to industrial growth.

Commentary

Henry C. Wallich

An effective society is a functional society. Institutions, including the institution of profit, must justify their existence by performing a function. A society cluttered up with obsolete remnants of history or burdened by special privilege is not effective.

Profits have been denounced by some as relics of the past and as a privilege for a few. I regard profits as functional. Fundamentally, I see them performing three functions. They allocate resources, by stimulating production of what is profitable and discouraging what is not. Profits also serve as a standard of performance, by rewarding the efficient and weeding out the inefficient. Finally, profits serve as a source of financing. Today, I believe, we are witnessing a change in the relative weight accorded these functions. Profits as a source of financing are becoming more important. Profits as a means for allocating resources seem to be losing some of their effectiveness. The first part of my observations will be concerned with this shift.

For the first time in a generation, American corporate business has been facing serious problems in financing its continued growth. Grow we must, if we are to have more jobs and higher living standards. But until recently, corporations financed this growth by shifting away from internal and toward external sources of funds, away from equity financing and toward debt, and away from long-term debt toward short-term debt. These trends have produced financial structures that make additional financing difficult.

Now the process must be reversed. We need more internal financing, a larger equity component in external financing, and consolidation of short-term debt into long-term debt as well. Profits play a role in all these adjustments.

It is useless to argue that if internal cash flow is inadequate and the stock market is not receptive to equity issues, business should just continue to borrow. This advice is like Queen Marie Antoinette's "Let them eat cake." Where there is not enough profit, there will be no equity financing; and where there is not enough equity, there will not be much debt money available. An adequate flow of profits is the basis for debt financing, equity financing, and, of course, internal financing.

A year or two of good profits, to be sure, will not immediately change corporate balance sheets. This would be true even if, as I expect, corporations will be prudent in raising dividends and will allow most of their growing profits to remain in the business. But even though, over a short span, book value of equity may not be greatly enhanced even by good earnings and cautious dividend policies, market value may well be. In a judgment of the debt capacity of a firm, it is the market value of the equity rather than its book value that counts primarily. Financing was relatively easy during the middle 1960s because the market value of equity exceeded book value by an average of almost 50 percent. New financing became more difficult in the course of 1974, when the first time in more than 20 years the market value of equity fell well below book.

I am aware of the argument that corporate restraint in dividend payments contributes little to aggregate saving because stockholders, receiving a smaller share of the earnings in the form of cash than they might like, can sell stock, and thus consume as much as they would have, had dividends been higher. I see the logic but I doubt the importance. The concept of total return, which would prompt stockholders to treat capital gains like dividends, has suffered a serious setback in the wake of market developments in the last few years. Lower dividends probably would mean less stockholder consumption and more aggregate saving. In short, it seems to me that profits, both directly as a source of funds and indirectly as a basis for equity and debt financing, are acquiring an increasingly important role.

Meanwhile, however, the role of profits in allocating resources is threatened by some recent developments. The reason lies both in factors that limit the profits which market forces otherwise produce and in other factors that enhance business risk.

Profits in particular industries today are affected by quasi-political decisions, such as requirements for environmental protection and controls affecting the price of oil, natural gas, and electric power. Whatever the merits of these decisions, their consequences are that profits are lower and that less investment is flowing into these areas than might be the case if resources were allocated according to a market-determined return on these investments.

A few years ago, new techniques of institutional investment within the stock market threatened to produce adverse allocational effects. I refer to the practice of "tiering," which bestowed upon a small number of seemingly fast-growing corporations a special status, giving them very high price/earnings multiples and hence a very low cost of capital. Meanwhile, the great majority of American equities were neglected by portfolio managers, raising the cost of capital to those firms. In the last year or two, the forces of the market have tended to bring about their own correction, leading to significant changes in investment philosophy. There is hope, therefore, that defective resource allocation resulting from these unbalanced portfolio policies may be a thing of the past.

Floating exchange rates may have a distorting effect on investment decisions in situations where such movements are larger than justified by underlying fundamentals. Moreover, the risk of investing for sale to foreign markets may rise under such conditions. Business may find it safer to invest in the market for which it is producing, in order to be assured of reasonably stable cost/price relationships. However, in a world in which movements of exchange rates do reflect fundamentals, resource allocation should be improved, as contrasted with a world of unrealistically fixed rates.

Let me turn now to the general behavior of businessmen with respect to profit. Students of economics are informed by their instructors that economic analysis is facilitated and the prospect of reaching determinate conclusions enhanced if it is assumed that firms try to maximize profits, even though they probably do not. There are, indeed, several other decision guides that firms may follow. They may, for instance, prefer to maximize sales or market share while striving for profits that are merely satisfactory because this enhances the prestige of the firm and perhaps of the executives. Alternatively, businesses may maximize utility, in which case they may sacrifice some profit while aiming at greater safety, which partly may take the form of high precautionary profit margins. Sometimes such differences in behavior are said to be associated with the difference between owner management and professional management.

The empirical evidence is slim. But to a casual observer, a great change seems to have come upon the corporate scene from the attitudes of the late 1960s and early 1970s to those induced by the subsequent recession and still visible today. This observable change in attitude seems consistent with the hypothesis that during the earlier years the dominant corporate style was to maximize sales at the expense of profits, while now it has become the style to stress safety and high margins. Corporate inventory policy, fixed-investment policy, hiring policy, policy with regard to financial structure, and profit margins all seem to point in that direction.

Such a shift, aside from its theoretical interest, could have far-reaching consequences. Maximizing sales and market share in the short and intermediate run means investment with comparatively lower capital intensity capable of providing large numbers of jobs. Maximizing utility, in the form of accent on safety, may mean investment for cost reduction rather than expansion, as well as perhaps less investment in the aggregate. Fewer jobs would be the consequence probably of the first and certainly of the second of these factors. For the longer run, of course, such fashions in corporate style are apt to alternate and be mutually self-correcting.

For our present situation, I would draw the conclusion that there are latent expansionary forces that could be released as business styles change once more in a direction of diminished risk aversion.

To be sure, the ability of business to move from the attenuated profit margins of some recent years to the better margins currently experienced raises questions concerning competitive structure. Before jumping to the conclusion, however, that a shift to higher profit margins represents a massive display of market power, I would like to note that the widening of margins appears to be a very general phenomenon. No great market power may in fact be required to expand margins when large numbers of firms are acting simultaneously in response to a reevaluation of risk.

Having said a number of things about profits and how they have moved down or up, let me pause for a moment to inquire how well we are able to measure profits at all. The Department of Commerce has made the computation of economic profits one of the principal features of its long-awaited comprehensive revision of the national income and product accounts. The major conceptual change has been to put depreciation on a consistent and replacement cost basis. Restated in this form, and excluding as before inventory profits, economic profits turn out to have been lower than previously believed, with the exception of a few years during the early 1960s. This is especially true of the last few years.

Contrasting with this Department of Commerce approach, which I regard as very constructive, is a proposal made by the Financial Accounting Standards Board (FASB). Where the Department of Commerce aims, by implication, but not exclusively, at a restatement of profits that eliminates the effects of inflation, all-inclusive inflation accounting is the principal objective of the FASB approach. The FASB approach includes, in effect, the inflationary upward adjustments on inventory and fixed assets, i.e., the inflation-induced net capital gains, whereas the Department of Commerce approach ignores these, since capital gains do not constitute part of the GNP with which the Department is concerned.

There is still a third form of profit accounting which stresses book-value profits—which is that of the business which treats inventories on first-in-first-out (FIFO) basis and makes no adjustment for underdepreciation. The proportion of firms that abandoned FIFO during the last couple of years seems to have been substantial, but an informed guess is that it is still the predominant corporate accounting technique.

During a period of inflation, differences between the three methods can be large. The highest profits typically, although not always, are given by the approach which involves FIFO inventory accounting. The FASB technique frequently—although by no means always, since it depends on the net monetary position of the firm, i.e., essentially the degree of leverage—seems to produce a somewhat lower value. The most conservative valuation tends to be that which is produced by the Department of Commerce method.

Which of the three techniques—and, of course, there are still others—is most nearly "right"? I have no special competence to answer such a question, but I can refer you to the answer given by the market when inflation was at its peak. During the period of high inflation, stock market values were low. The market put little store, apparently, in the gains that many corporations had from their net debtor position (or, inversely, from the excess of their nonmonetary assets over their equity). Inventory gains, moreover, accruing as they did in illiquid form, were of little use to corporations and produced tax liabilities to boot. Thus the stock market's answer was that the techniques producing the higher profit values are not the right ones. It is remarkable, under the circumstances, that the shift to LIFO was not much more general than apparently it has been. It is remarkable also that many corporations apparently believed that the stock market would react negatively to a LIFO-induced reduction in profits despite the indisputable benefits of tax saving.

These uncertainties about how to compute corporate profits should make us cautious about any general statements concerning such broad matters as the rate of return on capital or the share of corporate profits in the GNP. These matters are further complicated by the fact that of late a larger share of corporate financing has taken the form of debt. A larger share of the return to capital has therefore tended to take the form of interest. This tends to reduce the share of profits in the GNP. Fairly impressive evidence has been produced, for instance by William Nordhaus, that during the late 1960s the return on capital declined severely. This, then, would have been the main cause of the drop in the GNP share of profits. This may well be a more fundamental view of the matter than my hypothesis that during this period firms tended to engage in maximization of sales rather than of profits. But we shall have to await further evidence in order to see whether the decline in the rate of return on capital will turn out to be a lasting phenomenon. Conceivably, the rate of return on capital may turn up again, in line with my hypothesis that corporate style has changed once more to emphasize profits and safety. The much-debated emergence of a capital shortage—which I see as a possibility as the economy approaches full employment—could also work to raise the return of capital.

With respect to the past, I would like to introduce two sets of data. Table 1 shows profits of nonfinancial corporations adjusted by the Department of Commerce method for inventory valuation and underdepreciation. It relates these adjusted profits to the equity of nonfinancial corporations, which in turn is adjusted for the rate of inflation, i.e., revalued in proportion to it. These data show a sharp decline in the rate of return on equity from the middle 1960s to the middle 1970s. In contrast to the series of book-value profits of nonfinancial corporations as a percentage of that sector's GNP, also shown in Table 1, however, the data on economic profits as a percentage of adjusted (average) equity do not indicate a declining trend for most of the period since World War II.

Instead of looking at corporate profits in terms of the return on corporate equity, we can also look at them in terms of the rate of return to the stockholder on the value of his stocks, as displayed in Table 2. This approach has been made famous by the finding of Lawrence Fisher and James Lorie, recently updated, showing the return on common stock from 1926 to 1975 to have been about 8.5 percent. This return includes, of course, capital gains as well as dividends during the period. When this calculation is adjusted for inflation, the rate of return drops to something like two-thirds of its nominal value. For the last 10 years, moreover, the real rate of return to the stockholder has been negative. By whichever approach, we always reach the same conclusion: profits of late have not been good.

Proposals abound for remedying this state of affairs through the tax system. Integrating corporate and personal taxation to end the double taxation of dividends, tax deductibility of dividends, and on the side of the investor, tax-free reinvestment of dividends are among the more prominent proposals. If the

Table 1
Profits of Nonfinancial Corporations
(Billions of Dollars)

Year	Profits after Tax[a,c]	IVA[a]	Capital Consumption Allowance Adjustment[a]	Adjusted Profits[a]	Average Equity[b]	Return on Average Equity (percent)	After-Tax Profits[a] Gross Nonfinancial Corporate Product[a,c] (percent)
1946	13.4	-5.3	-2.7	5.4	105.3	5.1	13.5
1947	18.3	-5.9	-3.3	9.1	123.6	7.4	15.3
1948	20.0	-2.2	-3.9	13.9	141.4	9.8	14.6
1949	15.6	1.9	-3.8	13.7	152.3	9.0	11.7
1950	21.6	-5.0	-3.9	12.7	164.8	7.7	14.2
1951	17.9	-1.2	-4.5	12.2	183.0	6.7	10.3
1952	16.0	1.0	-4.4	12.6	197.1	6.4	8.8
1953	16.4	-1.0	-4.0	11.4	208.5	5.5	8.4
1954	16.4	-.3	-3.2	12.9	218.7	5.9	8.5
1955	21.8	-1.7	-2.1	18.0	233.9	7.7	10.1
1956	21.8	-2.7	-3.0	16.1	257.2	6.3	9.4
1957	20.7	-1.5	-3.3	15.9	277.8	5.7	8.5
1958	17.5	-.3	-3.4	13.8	291.9	4.7	7.4
1959	22.3	-.5	-2.9	18.9	305.2	6.2	8.4
1960	20.3	.3	-2.3	18.3	316.6	5.8	7.3
1961	19.7	.1	-1.8	18.0	324.8	5.5	6.9
1962	23.1	.1	1.0	24.2	336.6	7.2	7.4
1963	25.5	-.2	1.9	27.2	351.4	7.7	7.7
1964	30.7	-.5	2.6	32.8	369.9	8.9	8.6
1965	37.2	-1.9	3.6	38.9	393.2	9.9	9.5
1966	40.0	-2.1	3.8	41.7	422.6	9.9	9.3

1967	37.7	-1.7	3.6	39.6	456.5	8.7	8.3
1968	38.3	-3.4	3.6	38.5	491.0	7.8	7.7
1969	35.1	-5.5	3.5	33.1	530.8	6.2	6.5
1970	27.9	-5.1	1.5	24.3	574.5	4.2	5.0
1971	33.3	-5.0	.5	28.8	619.4	4.6	5.5
1972	42.4	-6.6	2.7	38.5	672.3	5.7	6.3
1973	53.7	-18.4	1.6	36.9	740.7	5.0	7.1
1974	61.1	-38.5	-2.1	20.5	851.1	2.4	7.6
1975	59.6^e	-10.6^e	-5.1^e	43.9^e	968.6^e	4.5^e	6.7

[a]Source: Department of Commerce.
[b]Source: FRB Flows of Funds.
[c]Excludes repatriated profits earned by foreign subsidiaries.

Five-Year Period	Mean Return on Average Equity	After-Tax Profits: Gross Nonfinancial Corporate Product
1946-1950	7.8%	13.9%
1951-1955	6.4	9.2
1956-1960	5.7	8.2
1961-1965	7.8	8.0
1966-1970	7.4	7.4
1971-1975	4.4	6.6

Table 2
Average Annual Nominal and Real Rates of Return
(10-Year Holding Periods, 1926-1975)

10-Year Period	Average Annual Rate of Return[a]		10-Year Period	Average Annual Rate of Return[a]	
	Nominal	*Real*		*Nominal*	*Real*
1926-1935	5.9%	10.4%	1946-1955	16.2%	8.3%
1927-1936	7.9	12.2	1947-1956	17.9	14.4
1928-1937	0.3	3.9	1948-1957	15.9	13.4
1929-1938	−0.6	3.3	1949-1958	19.4	17.5
1930-1939	0.1	4.6	1950-1959	18.8	16.7
1931-1940	1.8	4.4	1951-1960	15.8	13.6
1932-1941	6.2	4.0	1952-1961	16.1	14.5
1933-1942	9.1	3.5	1953-1962	13.1	11.7
1934-1943	7.0	1.7	1954-1963	15.6	14.1
1935-1944	9.1	4.6	1955-1964	12.6	8.8
1936-1945	8.2	4.1	1956-1965	10.9	9.2
1937-1946	4.3	−3.8	1957-1966	9.0	7.2
1938-1947	9.3	−0.2	1958-1967	12.6	10.9
1939-1948	7.0	−3.4	1959-1968	9.8	7.9
1940-1949	8.9	−1.9	1960-1969	7.7	5.3
1941-1950	13.0	2.1	1961-1970	8.0	5.1
1942-1951	16.8	6.9	1962-1971	6.9	3.7
1943-1952	16.6	8.3	1963-1972	8.1	6.3
1944-1953	13.9	5.9	1964-1973	5.9	1.9
1945-1954	16.6	8.4	1965-1974	1.2	−4.1
			1966-1975	3.7	−2.9

[a]Rates of return estimated using Standard and Poor's 500 stock index. Dividends assumed to be reinvested at year end.

	Nominal	Real
Mean	9.9	6.4
Standard deviation	5.4	5.4
Maximum	19.4	17.5
Minimum	−0.6	−4.1

nation is of a mind to recognize the functional importance of corporate profits by insisting on legislation of this type, I believe the economy would benefit. But all these proposals make income distribution more unequal. I should be surprised if much tax legislation improving the position of corporations and their stockholders were passed as long as the average person responding to surveys believes that profit margins on sales are 33 percent.

But as I have repeatedly noted, the tax law could be restructured to favor corporate profits and improve corporate financial structure without increasing the share of capital in the aggregate. This could be done by reducing the tax deductibility of interest, which would increase the corporate tax base, and by lowering the tax rate on corporate profits, so as to leave the overall corporate tax burden unchanged. The problems of shifting from our present system to that described could, I think, be dealt with by appropriate phasing-in measures.

A tax reform of this kind would, I think, be helpful. Even more important would be a change in national attitudes toward profits. At the present time, there still is widespread public misunderstanding of the relative share of profits. There is little understanding also of how large a part of the profit share goes for corporate and individual taxes and for corporate and individual saving and investment, and how small a part contributes to inequality of living standards. But a more constructive national attitude is in the making, I believe, thanks in part to evidence that profits are not only the lifeblood of trade but, more particularly, also of corporate financing. To this more constructive attitude, I hope, our meeting is making a contribution.

3

Why Profits Are Challenged

Kenneth J. Arrow

There are three concepts that are closely linked together but must be distinguished. For some problems, they are interchangeable; but for others, the differences are important. They are the concepts of private property, property income, and profit.

I point first of all to the concept of private property itself. Obviously it is not easy to imagine a profit system in the sense that we usually think of without private property, although profits, as I will enlarge on later, can be used as a measuring device in a society where property in the sense that we know it in this country does not exist. The ability to own property—particularly in the modern sense, which means the ability to alienate it, to sell it to others freely—is clearly and closely related to the operations of any kind of profit system; at least it constrains very severely the nature of the profits. Associated with property in a system in which property and its fruits are saleable is the concept of *property income*. Among forms of property income, one is the category of profits which has been the focus of this set of lectures. There are other forms: one can lend out one's property to others to employ productively and receive income in a form of rental or interest depending on the nature of the transaction. We figure profits primarily as a residual item, where the owner of a property uses it in a way which leaves him bearing the risks and deriving the benefits from possible fluctuations in the conditions of his trade and the prices he receives and pays. It is implied, then, that the resource-allocation decisions of society are made proximately by profit recipients, although under the constraints imposed by the rest of the system.

Challenges to the Roles of Profits: Private Property and Property Income

I want to discuss some challenges to the role of profits that have arisen in society from economists and from different intellectual groups. Some of the challenges are objections to all forms of property income, and some are objections to the idea of private property. Others discuss more specifically the possibility of using profits as a guide to action and the criticism thereof. Perhaps basic to most of the criticisms of profits is the fact that property income as such is a suspect category of return. Professor Samuelson alluded to this earlier today when he spoke of the sweat that is incurred or the lack thereof. This critical attitude is very ancient and can be found abundantly in the Bible. We may all recall the attitudes of the fourteenth-century English peasants who went reciting the jingle of the radical priest, John Ball: "When Adam delved and Eve span, where then was the gentleman?" The ideological view that earning your keep—digging of the ground, the production of clothing—is justly rewarded while people who do not engage in work are not entitled to a reward is one that recurs throughout history, and with special force in recent centuries.

One particular form that this attitude has taken is the prohibition of usury. The idea that there is something very objectionable about taking money for the use of one's property, particularly one's money or liquid property, which seems even one step further removed from real productivity, is very ancient indeed. Usury does raise an interesting issue for our purpose because typically profits were regarded in this context as a superior, not an inferior, form of property income. The same medieval tracts which ran to great lengths as to what was and was not usury did not prohibit trading; making a profit on trading was regarded as legitimate in a sense that usury was not.

Among the economists, especially in the modern period beginning with that much-referred-to gentleman Adam Smith, we find some feeling about the need for justifying profits, not so much in Smith or Ricardo themselves, but in Nassau Senior's concept of abstinence; but it is true, as Professor Samuelson reminded us by quoting Lassalle, that somehow the people who earn profits or other property are not characteristically "sacrificing" a great deal, at least as that term is ordinarily thought of. They are, from an economist's point of view, indeed abstaining from present consumption with a view of future reward, and to that extent it is a utility sacrifice. But in a world where on the whole the receipt of profits is associated with an already existing accumulation of property, the moral force of this argument, as opposed to the economic force, is not very impressive. That these feelings are in fact widespread among people, sometimes stronger, sometimes less, can, for example, be exemplified by the spread of Marxist ideas among the European working class in the last quarter of the nineteenth century. (There were other radicals with similar ideas, but the Marxists eclipsed their rivals and established something of a monopoly in this field.) The opposition to property income obviously persists to this day on the Continent in the form of the large and steady votes for Communist parties and in England in the non-Marxist form of steady adherence of the working class to the Labor party.

So we must recognize that this suspicion of property income, and profits as a part of that, must be reckoned with as a basic historical reality.

A somewhat different, though related, criterion by which property income is at least judged dubious is the demand for equality. Without going too far back in history, we find in the late eighteenth century an interesting intellectual development. The radical demands for civic equality and political equality—the abolition of distinction between the bourgeois and the nobleman—required justification, an elaboration by social theorists of a philosophy which would justify equality. An egalitarian philosophy spilled over in many ways into a demand for economic equality, already evidenced in small ways in the seventeenth- and eighteenth-century revolutions. We have the Diggers and Levellers in England and the followers of Babeuf and Buonarotti in the French Revolution. The philosophical needs for consistency made it very hard to justify political equality without leading to a demand for economic equality. I am thinking particularly of the utilitarian viewpoint as started by Bentham. Striking evidence can be found in the elaborations of utilitarianism by the economist Edgeworth toward the latter part of the nineteenth century. Edgeworth took the utilitarian philosophy very seriously and developed its implications at considerable length. It is perfectly obvious in his writings that he was very conservative and did not like equality at all, but he found himself driven by his logic to deducing egalitarian concepts of income distribution which were quite unpleasant to him. He then proceeded to blunt his implication on the matter by inventing all sorts of ingenious counterarguments. But he was an honest man and did not suppress these results.

The utilitarian school started from the principle that it is desirable to increase people's satisfaction as individuals. This was a rallying cry, a weapon for destroying privileges which could not be defended as enhancing people's satisfactions more or less as they judged them. Since everyone had to count as one and only one in Bentham's terms, the utilitarian principle took the form, to use slightly mathematical language, of maximizing a symmetric function—a function by which people were not labeled—and therefore, the outcome was very likely to be symmetric. In choosing an income distribution according to utilitarian principles, it is hard to wind up with anything but an equal income distribution.

Now it is obvious, empirically, at any rate, that profits certainly add to the inequality of income, and therefore a demand for equality does involve, among other things, an attack on profits and, in fact, on property income in general. It is a fact (maybe not a necessary truth, but certainly an empirical fact) that property and the receipts therefrom are more unequally distributed than earnings from labor. Actually, the popular perception probably exaggerates the point rather than minimizes it. I think that most people who have not looked at statistics will not realize the extent to which there is inequality in labor incomes and the degree to which the overall inequality of income is, in fact, an inequality of what is at least classified for income tax and statistical purposes as labor income. There are some problems of distinguishing these two when you get to the higher management levels. But even though there is an exaggeration, there is no question of the validity of the proposition that profits and property income statistically add to the inequality of income. Therefore, an egalitarian policy will tend to hit, to a rather considerable extent, at property income.

This brief statement of the suspicions about property income must be balanced by a recognition that there is also a great deal of acceptance of the legitimacy of property income among the populace and even among intellectuals, who frequently try to give a theoretical defense. There are various reasons why property could be accepted. Part of it is undoubtedly the fact that the status quo always has an edge in justifying itself. It *is*, after all, and anything else involves a change. It has been shown to work in some fashion or another in a way that we are accustomed to, and there is also some kind of perception that whatever a person has ought not to be taken away.

At least in the past, and I think probably to some considerable, unrealized extent today, religious belief has undoubtedly played a role also in justifying property income. In one interpretation—not the only possible one—it tends to justify the status quo because the world is presumably the working out of the divine will on earth, and therefore interference with it is somehow a source of blasphemy. There is a Church of England hymn which praises the divine order which has placed "the rich man in his castle, the poor man at his gate."

In addition to these subconscious defenses based on inertia or religion, there has been an intellectually more formidable defense of property income in general and profits in particular based on rather more secular considerations. One point of view is to meet head on the question of the legitimacy or justification of property income. This line of argument goes back at least to John Locke. It is argued that property, after all, derives ultimately from labor. Essentially, it is thought that an individual by his own labor, either working for himself or for others, earns but consumes less than he could. He has saved with a view toward future consumption, and therefore, in some sense, all property income is simply income redistributed in time. The fact that some individuals later are able to earn money from this merely reflects a justifiable contract made, so to speak, at the beginning.

This argument does not seem to cover the case of inheritance. Even here, though, there have been ingenious defenses; I found one in the writings of Lewis Carroll. This is an uncharacteristically serious passage, where he argues that, after all, if an individual has accumulated property legitimately, he has obviously the right to consume it; if instead of consuming it he chooses to leave it to his heirs, it is hard to see why this is a less legitimate method of spending his money. The argument shows that the idea of equality needs clarification; equality among earners is a different criterion than equality among consumers if the two groups are identical. Philosophically, it raises a question I am not going to address: Just when is an individual a separate individual? But in any case, even on its merits, Lewis Carroll's defense is not totally adequate; too many examples are known of profits derived from fraud, force, government favoritism, and corruption. Even when these factors did not intervene, there certainly seems frequently to be a great disproportion between the payoff in property and the labor or whatever input it is that ultimately justifies it. It is a little hard to see how some families like the Rockefellers in the nineteenth century could accumulate a billion dollars merely by hard work and thrift.

A basically different argument has been evolved by economists. It already appears in its essential form in Adam Smith and was developed by the late nineteenth-century economists. The argument is that really extraordinary incomes are profits rather than the more mundane forms of property income, like rents and interest, which tend to bear what might be thought of as a reasonable relation to the input. It is argued that these extraordinary profits are the results of successful risk bearing and are balanced by the losses of the unsuccessful. This argument has a certain appeal, but a limited one, because it amounts to justifying profits as having the same legitimacy as winnings at gambling tables. These are frequently not regarded as thoroughly respectable, although attitudes vary; in England, for example, winnings at the football pools are not taxed, and this differentiation could be regarded as signifying that they have even higher legitimacy than working for a living. No doubt, the rare winner in the gambles is looked up to by his friends, but the idea of a system in which sharp differentiations in income are largely due to luck lacks something in the way of good moral appeal.

Economists have also developed a different argument and one that does not necessarily lead to precisely the same conclusions. It is a special case of the justification of a price system, namely, that the use of society's resources is made more efficient by making sure that the user realizes and takes into account the cost of production or the value of the resource in alternative uses. Assets are useful in production, but they are scarce. Their employment therefore must be paid for in order to make sure that they are used in the most productive applications. Hence the use of property has to be priced. This justification of the charging of price for the use of property is not necessarily an argument that the reward should go to the owner rather than to someone else. In a private property system, it becomes very reasonable that the collector of the price, at least in the first instance, should be the owner of the property. It is essentially convenient that they do so, and it would hardly make sense to speak of property if the owner did not have this right. However, it does not follow without further argument that property income should not be taxed.

Profits in the residual sense are rather harder to justify on efficiency grounds than property income in general. The very fact that they are residual and the assumption that there is a considerable amount of randomness in the return imply precisely that the incentive effects are blunted in many ways as compared with the incentive effects of a sure return on the income. Probably the strongest argument for profits in the strict sense of the term as improving the efficiency of the economic system is Schumpeter's argument that the possibility of profits is the incentive to innovate and therefore that the role of profits is to encourage the development of new ideas and new uses for property.

Let me turn from these arguments of legitimacy of property income and of profits in particular to a broader issue, the justifiability or desirability of a system of private property. As already suggested, there is an inextricable correlation in economic systems between the existence of profit and the existence of private property in the particular form where it has the flexibility and alienability that it possesses in a modern economy—where it can be bought and sold freely through the market, as it could not in a feudal system or a system where a great deal of property is tied up, as in entail. In a regime of freely alienable private property, an individual has the choice of renting his property or using it himself in production. One of the implications of the "right of property" is precisely the right to make that decision. If in fact an individual uses his property in production, he can alienate the product rather than the property itself. That is to say, he is using the property to earn profits, if possible.

Let us think a minute about a world in which all values are available for purchase and sale. When in the early nineteenth century such a world became conceivable for the first time, many thinkers rebelled at the implications. When I was at the University of Chicago, some 25 years ago, the students put on a set of satirical sketches, one of which had as its main character the Rational Economic Man. He made no decision without carefully consulting his slide rule (this was before the days of pocket computers, you understand). He was finally asked what price he would charge for murdering his grandmother. He thought about it for a minute, made some computations, and then looked up to ask, "Do I have the right to sell the body?" Even in Chicago, the indoctrination was not 100 percent complete.

In a world where property is bought and sold and in which a profit system is operating, it is inevitable that human services be bought and sold. There is really no way of arranging it otherwise. Human services—labor in its most generalized sense—are disposed of by sale to individuals owning other assets or possibly used by the worker himself in cooperation with his own assets. Labor is not used in the form of voluntary cooperation or in that of conventional or legally enforced obligations. There is no question that these market arrangements contribute strongly to efficiency, and they have doubtless made a good deal of difference in our economic history. But what about the effects on human relations in face-to-face groups at the work place? The social feelings that we ordinarily expect to accompany working together are considerably shorn of their strength when the relation is contractual, terminable by any party when there is the slightest economic advantage in doing so. In a world dominated by the property system, the relations, which are the stuff of which society is made, are greatly affected by pure economic advantage. With every cooperative effort, there is always in the back of the mind the calculation "Is this worth it?" When the remnants of feudalism were being broken at the end of the eighteenth century, contemporaries saw the new era as one not only of liberty but also of fraternity. You might recall the words of Schiller's "Ode to Joy," which Beethoven set to music: when the bounds of custom are broken, then *"alle Menschen Brüder werden"* ("all men shall brothers be"). But the same changes appeared to Beethoven's contemporary, Burke, in a slightly different light. "The age of chivalry [goes a famous quotation] is dead. The age of sophists, calculators and economists is upon us, and Europe is the poorer."

Burke's views were continued by many nineteenth-century figures. Thomas Carlyle wrote critically, not to say hysterically, about the cash nexus and indeed about the dismal science. Perhaps surprisingly, his influence on Marx and Engels showed up in a famous passage in the *Communist Manifesto* which said that all the idyllic pastoral relations of feudalism were drowned in the icy calculation of capitalism. The preference for precapitalist social relations has remained a constant thread of conservative thought. There was a quite impressive though now semiforgotten literature in the 1930s by Elton Mayo and his colleagues at the Harvard Business School and by Lloyd Warner in his anthropological study of Newburyport in which the evils of the modern world (to exaggerate somewhat) were attributed to the lack of stable relationships, the destruction of the previously existing joys of community and craftsmanship, and their replacement by purely cash bonds. More recently we have heard almost exactly the same arguments, from the Marx-Engels rather than from Carlyle side, but the agreement is clear. The term *alienation* has become one of the most widely and excessively used terms of the ordinary man on the street and especially in the jargon of the undergraduate.

I do not want to leave the impression that the chilling effect of the universal property system, real though it is, is the only significant effect even apart from efficiency gains. The property system looks a little better when compared with possible alternative systems. It may be just a matter of one's personality, but speaking for myself, the idyllic quality sometimes ascribed to well-defined class structures with retainers humbly and joyously tugging their forelocks in the presence of the lord escapes me. There is a great gain in freedom, at least for the individual, at the expense of the social group; anonymous relationships of the market permit mobility and a real chance to expand horizons.

Apart from considering the defects of the alternatives, it must also be recognized that the property system is never universal. Social relations do intrude in all economic systems, and this fact raises questions about the role of profits that I want to come back to a little later.

Pragmatic Challenges: Unemployment and Price Inefficiencies

Let me now turn to a different set of challenges to the profit system, the pragmatic objections. How does the system in fact work, as opposed to objections based on general moral or sociological principles. There has been one basic flaw in the system almost from its inception: recurrent unemployment. Previous economic systems have all had their problems, but typically finding useful work to do was not one of them. Excessive work might have been a problem, as the ruling classes drove their slaves or serfs too hard; maldistribution of wealth, income, and consumption may also have been issues. Occasionally, labor might not have useful tasks because of a shortage of complementary factors, especially land. But that people should literally find nothing to do even when the other requisites for production are abundant is indeed a new phenomenon in world history. The possibility of unemployment is closely related to the profit-making motive and, in particular, to the decentralization which we in many respects regard as one of the virtues of the system. Shortages of effective demand become possible because there is no overall view which makes clear the unemployment of resources. An individual firm will decide to shut up shop or at least lay off workers when it is not selling its product. A self-contained manor would not have had that particular problem.

In every depression, the problem of unemployment rises to social consciousness. Early nineteenth-century discussions of the business cycle tended to be unsystematic until Sismondi and later Marx gave some rationalization. However difficult it may be for the scholar to trace exactly the relation between the theory of business cycles and the basic characteristics of the capitalist system, Marx at least made the connection. Many, not only Marxists, accepted the view that recurring unemployment was an intrinsic and ultimately fatal flaw of the system, so that dire predictions as to the future of capitalism appear to be justified every time we have a major depression.

The depression of the 1930s was of unprecedented magnitude and occurred in a world less willing to treat economic and social problems as inevitable than the less sophisticated nineteenth century. There was a fundamental intellectual shock to the system which has not yet been overcome. It is true that there is a new generation here which knows not the past, but the basic attack on self-confidence of defenders of the system is irretrievable. The system has responded by evolving, mainly in the direction of Keynes's thinking. One can assume that whatever the empirical and theoretical value of Keynesian economics may be, the fact that it offers a solution which on the one hand preserves many aspects of the system and on the other hand represents a major change was the key element in its acceptance. The doctrine of the invisible hand no longer had authority. An intrinsic role for intervention in the economy is a permanent feature, almost part of our orthodoxy rather than a doctrine held only by critics and outsiders in the system.

Keynesian doctrine has meant a basic change in the respect one has for the profit motive. It fails lamentably in one important way and can only be sustained by relatively artificial measures—deliberate manipulation of effective demand working through the profit motive to expand outward. Profit incentives may still be a useful auxiliary tool but no longer the all sufficient engine that had been envisioned in previous intellectual efforts.

A second pragmatic objection to the profit motive is more sophisticated. In fact it is one that economists dwell on more than other citizens. This is the idea that there is likely to be inefficiency in the allocation of resources because any price system to which profits are so closely related is likely to be incomplete. I refer of course to the question of externalities. We have now become very sensitized to environmental issues, which are in fact the issues arising when individual decisions have social consequences which are not properly priced or costed. When I drive my car into the central city, I am slowing everybody else down and that is a cost imposed on all the people which I do not pay. We are all now familiar with the uncompensated costs imposed on others by smoke-source pollution and the inefficiency created thereby. The price system is not in fact functioning in the way it is supposed to function. It is not in fact causing the user to understand the costs he is imposing on society.

Since output and input decisions are made by profit recipients, it is appealing to say loosely that profit seeking causes environmental damage. Actually, from a more sophisticated point of view, this is not quite the whole story; hard-working wage earners may in fact also find a cost imposed upon them by efforts to solve the problem of pollution. But in a profit economy, profits are the direct determinant of changes, and everything else ultimately derives from them. The legitimacy of profits when they are in fact derived from social bads rather than social goods is surely questionable. Externalities are not the only example of divergence between private profits and social benefit. The desire to monopolize is an intrinsic feature of a profit system—the profit recipient seeks to increase his profits in any way possible, and monopoly is one of them. But monopoly does not promote efficiency.

Thus in two basic respects, profit-driven economies do not achieve the end of efficiency. One is the repeated and costly failure to reach full employment, a very conspicuous kind of misallocation. The other is the incompleteness of the price system, whereby actions may lead to private good though social ill.

Are Profits the Basic Motive?

Finally, I would like to return to the point raised briefly earlier: that because no property system can be truly universal, profits are not the motive that drives everything. One can even ask very seriously, as has been done by many critics of standard economic theory in recent years, Is it in fact true that profits are the basic motive of the firm? Defenders of profits argue that in spite of the qualifications about employment and efficiency, the present economic system is satisfactory and therefore we need profits because profits drive the system. But what if profits are not the major motivation? There are many arguments along this line, but perhaps the most familiar one is that originated by Berle and Means some 40 years ago: that most large corporations are run not by the people who receive the profits, the stockholders, but by the managers. The stockholding is too splintered for the stockholders to have any effective control. The managers receive a relatively small fraction of profits; as stockholders, they characteristically have a half of 1 percent or 1 percent of the total stock outstanding. Therefore, it is not clear why they should want to maximize profits. The managers may well want to maximize other goals, perhaps their job perquisites or their control over the corporation.

There is another hypothesis which implies a divorce between profit seeking and business decisions, one that goes back in some ways to Thorstein Veblen. Many decisions are being made, not by the top management, but generally by middle management. In particular, development of new ideas in production and product is directed by the technologists. These engineers may typically have different motives than maximizing profits. They are interested in technique for its own sake. It is technical efficiency rather than business efficiency that they are trained to seek. Veblen himself thought that business efficiency, the maximization of pecuniary profits, was a bad thing; he assumed that the participation of engineers was improving efficiency. But the opposite might be maintained: that there is too much desire for novelty in technology. This strand of argument has been developed by several writers over the last 20 years, most notably by my colleague, John Kenneth Galbraith. The motives of the firm become essentially its self-preservation, its growth, its ability to innovate rather than its maximization of profits.

Hebert Simon and his colleagues at Carnegie-Mellon University have come to similar conclusions with a rather different argument: in a complicated organization it is impossible to maximize profits. It is just too hard to know what is going on. When there are so many decisions to be made, any central group will simply be overloaded with information and will not be able to handle the decision making. Once the overload is relieved by decentralization within the firm, the actual decision makers have many motives other than the maximization of profits.

These arguments have not gone unanswered, although it is hard to find a forum where the controversy about business motivation is well carried on. It is certainly established that in a great part of American industry, and probably an even larger portion of industry in other countries, the decision makers have the opportunity to depart from profit maximization, at least in the short run. Those who actually receive the profits simply do not have the power to control the firm, and therefore it would appear they do not have the power to bring the profits up to the maximum level. A manager can operate a firm in ways different from those called for by profit maximization. The usual hypothesis, although not the only one, is that managers want their firms to be bigger. They want their firms to survive and to grow—and growth is, of course, different from maximization of profits. It would seem that managers would strive to make their firms larger than is optimal for profitability.

This is not the occasion to go into details, but there is considerable evidence that the implications of the growth-maximization hypothesis are not quite what the proponents have thought. If a firm wants to grow, it had better have profits in order to engage in growth. In general, it appears that in a profit system, carrying out almost any management plans requires profits and therefore some incentive to maximize them. It is also true that in a world where profits have been taken as the criterion of success, the motive of the managers, if measured in self-esteem or social status, may well be the maximization of profits. The matter is not easily subject to any genuine proof, but much informal evidence would tend toward the view that profit is certainly a major consideration in management decisions, although the decisions need not be in the narrow, private interests of the managers.

However, to the extent it is true, this proposition has another damaging implication for the profit system. It means that the present economic system is working by the criterion of maximizing profits but not by receipt of profits. There is a big difference between profits as a signal, as a motive which allocates resources, and profits as a source of income. It is in this context, I think, that one might think of different economic systems in which the concept of profits plays the same measuring role it does in our system (or, perhaps I should say, in an ideal textbook version of our system), but in which income distribution is divorced from the workings of the price system as an allocative mechanism and, in particular, from the workings of the profit system as part of that mechanism.

There is another argument against the usefulness of profits as a motivating force. Its importance is not easy to assess, but I think it may not be inconsiderable. To a considerable extent, profits, from the point of view of the individual firm, are gained by a competitive advantage rather than by a social benefit. Professor Samuelson alluded to this very briefly this morning when he spoke of the advantage of being a minute or two ahead of your competitor. It may be that a new product could be introduced by many firms. Nevertheless, the one that introduces it first may have a large advantage. That particular reward is of relatively little consequence socially. If you think of the proper social reward to an individual from the point of view of efficiency as being the difference his existence makes to society, then in a situation like this it may well be that no individual is of any particular importance. The only social advantage conveyed by the individual who happens to get there first is the value of the short additional period of time the product is available as compared with that of the second earliest introducer. That value is usually trivial. Yet the economic advantage to the individual may be very disproportionate. There may be a considerable amount of overinvestment of resources in competitive information gathering. Where it would quite suffice from a social point of view to have one group doing research or developing a new product, you may have 50 groups doing it because each one will hope to derive this large advantage. Similarly, on speculative markets such as those for stocks and commodity futures, a large amount invested in the acquisition of new information for private advantage will yield no social gain, only a zero-sum redistribution. The redistribution of income through speculation may have two possible undesirable consequences. One is that it may lead to an increase in income inequality, in the sense that an individual who has some capacity for processing information slightly faster may get a very large competitive gain which has zero or very small social value. The second is that a large amount of resources may be invested in trying to achieve the redistribution with no social gain. We may have very able people who could be useful in production spending their time instead trying to outwit others.

The last few points have questioned the necessity of the profit system for a satisfactory economy. I have suggested that our economic system runs with profits as a signal but not entirely as a source of income; I have also suggested that some classes of profits, at least, are based on information-processing capacity and on employment of information that may have very little social value. To complete this line of argument, we must recognize that an economic system that does not work for profits may nevertheless operate, even with some degree of success. The fact is, in spite of the usual tendency to talk about the inefficiency of governments, that their record is by no means wholly bad; and of course, we all know the record of private industry is by no means wholly good. To take one perhaps very favorable example, the Manhattan Project (the development of the atomic bomb) would have been regarded as a supreme example of the superiority of a private enterprise system had it in fact been done by private enterprise. The Project represented a degree of sophistication in resource allocation in a very, very challenging set of circumstances and vast uncertainties that, I think, would be very hard to match anywhere. In fact, I still find its success somewhat inexplicable; and maybe the only reasonable hypothesis is that it happened to draw in a large number of extraordinarily able individuals motivated by a patriotic situation which may not easily recur. It was full of organizational innovations—especially the idea of parallel developments of alternative possible solutions—and many of the lessons of that experience seem to be completely ignored in almost all subsequent research and development work, whether by the government or by private industry.

The Tennessee Valley Authority (TVA) is something of which we have heard very little in recent years. What it seems to do is work as a reasonably efficient public utility, not remarkably distinguished among them, but by no means the rear. Yet it is run by people who by no stretch of the imagination derive any profit whatever from it. Truly managerial motivations, a simple motivation to do well, some but not too much fear of losing jobs in the absence of good performance, and the intrinsic rewards of running a large organization successfully seem not to be contrary to ordinary efficiency standards and can be maintained for a long period of time quite successfully.

If we look abroad, we do find that socialist countries can operate contrary to what a lot of economists would have thought and Ludwig von Mises, among others, said in the early 1920s. We now have whole societies (the Soviet Union, the Eastern European countries, China) in which a socialist economic system works. One can find plenty of deficiencies—I am not trying to extol these economies as supreme triumphs of economic efficiency—but these systems work with moderate degrees of economic success. By the usual criteria, they are, in fact, not doing badly, and this is particularly true in the industrial sector. Moreover, what problems they have experienced seem to have more to do with agriculture, where there is simply no substitute, not so much for the property system in general, but for direct mixing of the profit motive and the actual day-by-day managerial motive. But in the industrial sector, we find economies which are capable of progress, development, changing ideas, reasonable levels of efficiency, and growth, where not merely part of the system, as one of our large corporations, but the whole system is being operated without profits being a source of income to any individual.

I need no persuasion as to the negative political aspects of these nations, but they do refute the argument that even from a purely economic point of view, one could not have a viable socialist economic system.

This discussion concludes that profits have played a basic role in our economy, but that the challenge that we can erase the profit system is a very real one, compounded by underlying moral resentment about unearned income, by the coldness and deleterious effects on social relationships engendered by the universal property system, by the obvious failures of the economic system in unemployment and resource allocation, and finally, by the successful operation of non-profit-oriented societies and units within our own system.

Commentary

Arthur W. Harrigan

Professor Arrow has given us a well-balanced discussion of the challenge to profits and was generally bipartisan in his approach.

It will come as no surprise to you that my approach to this discussion is a totally partisan one. The 30 years I have spent in manufacturing enterprises have made me uniquely conscious of the price the investor demands for the capital that is needed for the bricks, mortar, and machinery of production. My own experience tells me that no investor will provide the capital for the machines to produce the telephone cables over which we communicate and no investor will provide the capital for the machines to produce the paper on which we also communicate without the conviction that those machines will earn a profit commensurate with what he perceives his investment risk to be. I know this to be true of the bondholders, for they demand that the firm to which they have loaned money have the prospect of earning profits amounting to several times the interest rate contractually due all creditors to minimize the risk that the bondholders will (1) not get their investment back and (2) will not receive their semiannual interest payments when due. I know it to be equally true of equity investors, for they demand a prospective profit stream from their investment sufficient (1) to pay dividends and (2) to generate market appreciation of the investment in recognition of retained and reinvested earnings which, in combination, will provide total returns commensurate with their risks.

Any examination of profits, their justification, and the challenges confronting the profit earner should start with the expectations of investors. I start here because each of us is an investor, with individual expectations regarding the rewards—or the profits—from our investment. The amount and character of economic activity that is generated are determined by our investment choices or the choices of those to whom we entrust our investment decisions. Whether we call it interest, dividends, or market appreciation, all of us expect to earn a profit from our deposits in savings banks, the government bonds we purchase, the industrial or utility bonds we buy, or the common stocks we choose—a profit whose rate varies with the risk of the investment. Even those who believe they are making no investment decisions are still profiting from the investment component of the insurance they buy or the pension funds to which they or their employer contribute. The investor in obligations of municipalities, truly nonprofit institutions, still seeks a reward commensurate with the risk; and if you question whether the expected reward is measured by the risk, I suggest you look at the "profit" rate on New York City securities. The only time we do not expect reward for our investment is when the investment is commandeered, as it is through the government's power of taxation, or when we voluntarily donate to our favorite church, charity, or academic institution. And even those institutions have to pay the investor's price if their benefactors are not sufficiently generous. Parenthetically, I should note that these same institutions, though clearly and properly nonprofit, are just as profit oriented as other investors when it comes to investing endowments and other surplus funds they might have.

I could go on talking about the supply or source aspect of investment and the interest every investor has in realizing a profit, but the major challenges to profits are directed at the profit generators—those who use capital dollars to acquire and operate the machinery of production to meet customer needs for goods and services. Thus I will shift from the *source* to the *use* side of capital investment as I get further into my discussion of why profits are challenged.

As Professor Arrow's paper suggests, the catalog of reasons why profits are challenged is a big one, and it is not easy to categorize them in mutually exclusive groups. Classification is made difficult not only because many of the reasons are related, but also because some of them are rooted in attitudes shaped by events which occurred in the distant past, in the absence of a conviction that those events will not recur. The aphorism "My mind's made up, don't confuse me with the facts" seems, regrettably, to reflect the attitude of many toward profits. Or perhaps it is just another case of making a virtue out of prejudice.

It is indeed a challenge to persuade an individual whose attitude has been shaped by accounts of the depredations of some of the nation's early entrepreneurs (such as those in the book *The Robber Barons*) that profits as rewards for economic contributions are as legitimate as the wages of labor, that profits are as much a cost of production as the materials that are consumed in the process, and that the expectation of profits spurs innovation and justifies the assumption of risk without which neither our society nor any other society, including communist nations, could hope to grow and prosper. Russia, regardless of its professed lack of profit orientation, still looks to us and to other developed nations for the technological and managerial leadership that is motivated and sustained by the recognition that profits are a reward for risk and for the innovation of which that risk is the essence.

Put another way, profits represent a standard measurement of efficiency and as such, a guarantee that our productive activities will be conducted in an efficient manner.

While I would not want to defend Rockefeller from Professor Arrow's suggestion that his fortune did not result from hard work, efficiency, and innovation, I would cite Henry Ford as a counterexample of one whose efficiency and innovation resulted in a profit to himself and to society—and that society still benefits from the foundation created out of his fortune of accumulated profits.

It would be a great misfortune for this country if the avarice of some of our entrepreneurial forebears caused us to lack confidence in profits as a prime mechanism for achieving the efficiency which nourishes our economy. It would be an even greater misfortune if the recent evidence of questionable business practices of a few led to condemnation of our entire private enterprise system. This is why I put engrained negative attitudes toward profits first among the reasons for the challenge to profits.

The second reason for the challenge to profits that I would like to list is the common practice of looking at them through a magnifying glass and concluding that they are many times their actual magnitude. You are all familiar with Opinion Research Corporation's survey released in early 1972 which reported that the average estimate of manufacturer's profits on each dollar of sales was 28 cents—this is more than five times the 5 cents the average manufacturer typically earns on each dollar of sales. Even stockholders, who should have greater knowledge about such things, also viewed profit rates through a magnifying glass: they estimated them to be 23 cents per dollar of sales.

Regrettably, the economic education programs that were accelerated in the face of such appalling ignorance seem to have had little effect on this exaggerated notion of the degree of profitability. In my own company, a recent survey among the employees produced an estimate of our profits of 29.3 cents per dollar of sales, or somewhat more than the 25.1 cents per dollar of sales they estimated all manufacturing firms earned. Our actual figure for 1974, one of our better years in recent history, was 8.6 cents.

Happily, though, this same group thought that the government got in taxes nearly as much from our sales dollar as they thought we earned in profits—26.7 cents for firms in the paper and forest products industry. Even more encouraging is the same group's views on what profits meant to them: Asked to react to typical statements which best expressed their views about companies and profits, 77 percent marked "growth and expansion of the business," while 70 percent mentioned "good wages and benefits." Statements such as "improved standard of living," "improved facilities and equipment to work with," and "improved working conditions" were given marks in the range of 50 percent. We may not have been successful in putting the magnitude of our profits in proper perspective, but we certainly have succeeded in establishing a positive attitude toward the role of profits among the majority of our employees. This offers some hope that the challenge to profits due to exaggeration of their amount may be less in the future.

There is no doubt in my mind that the public's overmagnification of profits is due to the use of absolute dollars of profit rather than the much more meaningful and correct relative measure—relative to the investment on which those profits were earned. General Motors and American Telephone and Telegraph Company are frequently headlined for being the largest profit makers in the country. The suggestion that their profits are fantastically large in amount is reinforced when the subheads tell us that the profits of one or the other of these companies exceeded the revenues of many nations throughout the world.

The impression that profits are high is frequently reinforced by big headlines when there are striking gains in year-to-year or quarter-to-quarter total dollars of profit and profits per share; special circumstances which may be responsible for such striking gains are seldom fully brought out. More important, we hardly ever see the profits expressed as a rate of return on all the capital dollars employed in the business, an omission that business firms have done little to correct. A relative measure of profitability is much more meaningful than an absolute one because it tells the investor how well the company is doing in managing all the assets entrusted to it, because it can be used in comparing one company's performance with another, and because it is one of the most commonly used measures within the business to evaluate new investment opportunities. In the final analysis, an investor in the business, whether through bonds or equity, is interested in the rate of return being realized and whether this rate of return is likely to cover his "price" for maintaining investment in the business.

As a final point in my commentary about profit exaggeration, I would note the contribution made by the Department of Commerce's national accounts reporting. When the information is released on the profit component of national income, the figures are impressively large, regardless of whether pretax or posttax figures are reported in the press. Only the professionals who analyze these figures recognize that corporate profits have not kept pace with compensation of employees, the major income component. As a result, profits as a percentage of the national income are much lower now than they were. For example, the record high level of pretax corporate profits in 1974 represented 11.6 percent of national income, a level significantly below that achieved in many years of the 1950s and 1960s. Again, a relative measure would put profits in proper perspective, and its more frequent use would do much to temper the challenges.

The concept that profits are a residual after all costs have been paid is another important reason for their challenge. This concept, which is attributable to the way accountants prepare financial statements, suggests that the below-the-line residual is not truly a cost of production in and of itself. Instead, this residual noncost element is what the entrepreneurs or the owners of the business can retain from the total income of the business after all costs have been met. Coupled with the tendency I have already noted to magnify the amount of profits, the residual concept easily leads to the view that profits are exploitative rather than a real cost of production that must be appraised on its economic merits. Unfortunately, this view is only a short step from Marx's theory of surplus value, in which labor is credited as the source of all value. I sometimes feel that many have taken this step without being fully conscious of it. I cite as an example the view that Professor Arrow discussed, that earning without work is immoral. Another example is the political view that money earned through labor should be subject to much less taxation than money earned on money.

The final challenge to profits that I would like to discuss is the view that profits seem to disappear when the operation is moved from the private to the public sector, and thus, profits are unnecessary to motivate efficiency and innovation or to reward risk. After all, the government can reduce or eliminate the risk. Professor Arrow discussed the question of whether profits are "a necessary motive," and he pointed to successful enterprises in the public sector, such as the Manhattan Project. As one who was in the Pacific in World War II, I hesitate to criticize the Manhattan Project since it may have saved my life. I would point out, however, that it was a "cost is no obstacle" wartime operation that simply is not comparable to the functioning of our economic institutions in peacetime.

With respect to the TVA, which Professor Arrow also cited as an example of an efficient nonprofit organization, this was the debating topic of the year back around 1938, and I thought that the argument about public versus private power generation had been pretty well settled. While I am aware that TVA has expanded from purely hydroelectric generation to coal-burning generation, I think it is significant that there has been no expansion of the TVA concept to other areas of the country.

I find no evidence that any socialist society which purports to remove the motivation of profit is as dynamic as our system. At the same time, people living in those societies lack our freedom. I believe that the U.S. Post Office is a grand example of what happens when there is no profit motive for efficiency. In addition, we do not have the freedom to take our postal business elsewhere. Abroad, we have the United Kingdom as a grand example of what happens when you shift enterprise from private to public sector. If you erase profits, you erase hope of efficiency.

Profits are not the main purpose of business, but like blood in the body, they assure that serving customers, which is the main purpose of business, is done most efficiently.

Commentary

C. Lowell Harriss

What does "the public" think about profit? Why? Does any appreciable significance really attach to popular attitudes about profit?

Opinion polls have documented popular views about the size of profit. Enormously wide of the mark, the general impression grossly exaggerates the amount. An ORC Public Opinion Index (April 1975) found the public estimating manufacturers' profits at 33 percent of sales compared with the actual of 5.2 percent in 1974—six times the actual. For auto manufacturers, the estimate was 20 times the reality at the time (a bad year); and for oil companies, over 8 times. A May 1975 Gallup report showed the median estimate by college students of profit as 45 percent of sales. Other surveys have also found enormous misconceptions. None that I can recall has found public estimates of profit in relation to sales or to capital to be other than far above reality. Have you ever seen a poll of attitudes about the frequency and size of loss? I know of none.

Acting on erroneous information, the public can adopt unwise policies. Avoidable mistakes bring needless harm. Will not the public be led to expect vastly more from corporations than can possibly be provided out of existing earnings? Today many new or expanded demands are pressed on business. The burdens of higher costs of government (taxes), rising outlays for environmental programs, the expenses of stricter safety and health standards, these and more seem to be expected, implicitly out of profit. Corporations are urged to make gifts to universities and the arts and for local betterment, to finance more expensive pension programs, to assure better warranties and in other ways reduce the likelihood of consumer dissatisfaction, to absorb higher costs of energy and develop new supplies, to pay higher wages, and also to hold the line on prices. Laws, regulations, union demands, and popular pressures put strains on the business system. The results will not all appear at once and may never be fully identifiable. But frustration and worse may follow from public expectations resting on widely exaggerated views about the amount of business profit and the role of profit and loss in the economic system.

Why do people believe profits to be so much larger than they are? Several reasons come to mind. The "man in the street" may think of gross returns to capital, failing to allow for interest, taxes, depreciation, and other expenses. In addition, profits become news most often during adversary proceedings in which someone wants to convey an impression that they are very large indeed, e.g., wage rate negotiations, utility rate proceedings, or when earnings are unusually high. Perhaps profit is sometimes confused with high executive compensation.

Corporations seem to report profit as a global total: one figure for the quarter or even full year. Frequently, such amounts are "large" enough to give an impression of something very big indeed. More meaningful reporting for most purposes would be earnings as cents per dollar of capital at risk or perhaps as cents per dollar of sales. Profit figures as reported embody two economic elements: the portion corresponding to *interest* and the payment for *risk bearing.* Implicit interest, economists recognize, is a cost of commitment of all capital, equity as well as debt. There should be a measure of sacrificed alternative, the interest that could be obtained from a debt investment. In the popular view, I expect, the term *profit* is associated with something above cost (as somehow conceived), but the figures published are not for that element alone. Figures of "profit" as 12 percent or so on net worth include in fact interest (implicit) of, perhaps, half that amount. So the reward for risk taking is markedly less than the figure shown for total return to equity capital.

Further, because of the impact of inflation, the traditional reporting of earnings has overstated actual results in recent years. Many corporations were laggard in utilizing LIFO accounting, so that true profits were overstated and taxes were greater than necessary. Depreciation also has been reported as less than corporate officers and their accountants must have recognized as realistic—again profits have been overstated. The total effects of inflation are not only complex for any one company, but differ widely from company to company. For example, the significance of inflation for the purchasing power of debt owned and held (the real burden or worth to be obtained) will generally be uncertain even when the fact of the existence of some distortion is undeniable.

Popular opinions about profit and its role in the economy come from many and diverse sources. Precise thinking, even clear definition, is rare. The "public's" views probably relate to those toward "business"—in itself a subject of vast breadth. If "antibusiness" views are spreading, attitudes toward profit are probably related. Yet, if one surveys the broad sweep of history, one finds that most of the major improvements in our standard of living have been developed and achieved by business, i.e., by profit-seeking enterprise, not governmentally operated "business." Those improvements which may be associated with government, i.e., with politics and bureaucracy, have often rested on tax revenues made possible by what we have accomplished in business. Profit has been a key element in the remarkable record of material progress. Yet skepticism and even condemnation of profit remain.

There are many possible explanations. First, some profit results from monopoly rather than serving as payment for the constructive service of equity capital. Monopoly certainly has elements to be condemned, but how large an element can genuinely continuing monopoly profit be when the total net return on equity of the leading corporations averages somewhat over 12 percent. The same company may receive profit from both use of monopoly power and constructive innovation and risk taking. And in real-world competition, few high-profit portions of a business, even with patent protection, can long maintain monopoly-level profits without providing the consumer with something more attractive or finding less expensive means of production.

Another argument is that profits may stem from such disreputable actions as skulduggery, deception, corruption, shady or illegal practices, and now, of course, bribery to make sales, and manipulation of governments at all levels. Because war, which represents human tragedy, has played a part in profit—and loss—the stigma of wartime profiteering may carry over to profit in general. Systematic information about the amount of pernicious activity can never be expected. Perpetrators will seldom advertise their actions. The cases which occasionally appear in the news offer no sound basis for judgment about the total of all business. The examples are probably trifling as a fraction of the billions of transactions each day.

The fact that chance, luck, and good fortune may bring profit—and their opposites bring losses—with no discernible evidence of justice may also warrant criticism. One may well agree and yet insist that at the most such sources of profit—and loss—account for very little of the total in the economy.

Marxian influence also exerts some sway over opinion. The employer, it is said, pays laborers less than the full value of what they produce. The difference is surplus value, profit, exploitation. (Are employees of companies making losses instead of profits exploiting the suppliers of capital?) But the Marxian assumption that nonlabor services are not productive should have no supporters in a world replete with evidence of the role of entrepreneurship and the worth of the provision of capital. Capital represents more than "congealed labor." Abstinence and saving, waiting, and risk taking, along with the labor which builds machines, are also essential in the supply of long-lived production capacity.

Some individuals and groups (occasionally religious groups) seem to feel that the search for personal gain is unworthy—and more unworthy, apparently, when called *profit* rather than *wages*. We hear criticisms of businesses for seeking profit, for putting this implicitly disreputable and presumably dispensable result of activity ahead of other "good things." The characterization "not for profit" is sometimes cited as implying some merit. Profit (and losses?) may also be criticized as accounting for some inequalities in wealth and income. And today some "intellectuals" put inequality very high on the list of things they do not like. Here the teaching of American history and literature in schools and colleges allocates irresponsibly greater attention to the "robber baron" approach than to the constructive achievements of businessmen and business. And news media today! How many allegations, irresponsible generalizations, and unsubstantiated assertions get broadcast without correction or "equal time" response?

(Losses, it seems to me, deserve more attention. Is there not something very much wrong in the company that is losing money? To the extent that someone hopes to encourage change to make a better world—and is this not the presumed intent of critics of profit?—will there not be greater hope for "doing good" by converting losing operations to profitable ones? Not, of course, by subsidies from taxpayers or restrictions on competition, but by improving the relation of desired output to input—by product improvement or more efficient production! Productive resources are not being used as creatively as in the economy generally. "What is wrong" must often be businesses operating unprofitably rather than those earning high profits. One characteristic of governmental (political) enterprise-type activities is that losses do not more or less automatically force discontinuation of operations.)

Despite these criticisms, the hope for profit and the fear of loss play vital roles in the economy, helping to force and to guide management to be economical. They provide drive for getting efficient allocation of resources, for preventing waste. We also willingly pay for the innovation and entrepreneurship that have results we welcome—new products or services and lower-cost methods of production. Professor Schumpeter emphasized entrepreneurship as a major source of profit. By no means are all efforts successful. Competition then eats away at this source of profit. New efforts must be made repeatedly—and successfully—to maintain a company's return on equity capital above a rather uninteresting "normal."

The desire to make profit, and to avoid loss, will continually have decisive influence on the allocation of resources. The profits actually realized indicate the industries and areas where additional resources and economic growth are most likely needed to serve human desires. Losses show where contraction is desirable. Profits and losses reveal which firms, which departments within firms, and to some extent, which methods are serving best and worst in economizing in the use of resources. Profits and losses do more than indicate, they also reward and penalize. In doing so, they provide funds which ease the way of those who have done well and withdraw resources from those who have done poorly.

Sometimes it is said (as at this conference) that giant corporations today are run by managers, and ownership is widely diffused. For such organizations is there really any need for profit as an "above normal" return on equity investment? The people who run these organizations have, at most, only tiny shares of the ownership. Perhaps bureaucracy governs. If opportunities are good, can new capital funds not be obtained equally well by borrowing or by reinvesting earnings? To what extent are the decisions of managers of big enterprises influenced by truly entrepreneurial motivations? Not many of us in academe know enough about the operations of even one or two large companies to feel competent to draw conclusions about the extent of entrepreneurial spirit.

However, in tests of performance, some big companies do much better than others. The quality of policy decisions which make real differences in results, as well as the quality of routine management, must reflect something more than accident. Perhaps the extent to which individuals who have influence over actions also have some direct interest in success or failure does account for some of the differences between good and poor results in even the largest corporations. Even though the managers may not own a big fraction of total equity capital, a large portion of their own individual economic interest may be tied to the company. Pension prospects, stock options, and profit sharing, as well as salary and security, can mean enough to executives, I expect, to instill more substantial entrepreneurial spirit.

Within the giant company there will be rivalry for capital for new undertakings—and these will have chances of success and failure ranging through a wide spectrum. If there were no profit-loss calculations, then how would divisions compete among themselves? How would losses be covered? Neither theory nor facts, to the extent that I know them, provide a basis for confidence in a judgment of economists that large established firms can dispense with hope of profit and fear of loss and still be run well. Neither the public utility model, with no true profit element, nor governmental operation, which would be "profit-loss neutral," offers enticing attractions.

My reading of economic history and my observations of the economy, both admittedly limited, suggest this conclusion: If a generation or a decade ago, America's most profitable manufacturers, retailers, financial firms, and service organizations had been "nationalized," if they had somehow been foreclosed from the prospect and the reality of profit above average, Americans today would have a sadly lower level of living. Not the least disadvantages would have been people now receiving services paid for by federal and state taxes.

Commentary

Russell E. Palmer

It is a privilege to share a platform with Professor Arrow. Prior to this I had only known him by the reputation of his powerful mind. After his presentation today, it is clear that his reputation is well justified. I am also pleased to be here with Arthur Harrigan and Professor Harriss. I think they have both given us a number of important insights.

All of us have different backgrounds and different perspectives on this challenge to profit, so we have opportunities to look at it from different vantage points. Those of you in the academic community teach and conduct research, and you also consult in live business environments. Those of you in business may be product or price oriented, but you also manage people. As an accountant, my job is to measure and report on that part of profit that we call *net income.* But I am a practicing businessman, so I also see another side. I am responsible for an enterprise that has 14,000 professional people in more than 50 countries depending on its operation. My job as a business manager is to ensure that we serve clients very well and, at the same time, achieve a level of shareholder profit consistent with our professional responsibility to the financial community and the public interest. My responsibilities as an accountant, and as a businessman, give me a different perspective on this issue of profit, and I would like to share some of my observations from that perspective with you.

First, let me agree that our traditional concept of profit has been subjected to challenge. (I certainly would not argue with what Professor Arrow has said about unemployment, business cycles, or environmental factors.) But the challenge to profit may be a challenge to our understanding and not to the fundamentals of the profit system. I am convinced that the system works, whether we like it or not. Profit, or the anticipation of profit, still motivates people.

In an organization of 14,000 professionals, you must know what motivates people or you have got a disaster on your hands. We do not make widgets; we do not have automated machines or assembly lines; and we do not take natural resources out of the ground. We have only one asset—people. The firm rises or falls on how those people tick. My experience convinces me that those who would be motivated by any stimulus are motivated most by the opportunity for profit.

It is true that the motivating power of cash return is tempered by inflation and our progressive tax structure. It is also true that professional accountants are trained to respond to client needs first and pecuniary rewards second. But let me define *profit* broadly. Profit can be the strengthening of the firm as a whole; it can be the growth of an individual unit within the firm and the pride and expectations of the individuals within the unit; or it can be the perceived success of an individual member of that firm. Every year we publish the results of the partnership, in total and by partner. The publication of the earnings book by partner is as important to most of the partners as is the actual distribution of the earnings. A relative improvement in the standings is an indication of current success, and an indication of opportunity for future challenge and growth.

Some say that profit motivates the mature man because he marches to an older, obsolete tune. I have heard, as you have, that today's young people are turned off by profit. We are often warned that the younger generation (and I included myself there a year or two ago) is not motivated at all or is motivated to a limited level of effort. As I have said, "people are our business," and it's critical that we understand them. After considerable study, and a number of inquiries, I have come away convinced that today's young people, properly challenged, are just as motivated and respond just as eagerly to an opportunity for personal success as any other generation that I have seen in my 20 years in business. I will acknowledge that in our recruiting we look for the motivated people, so my perception may be distorted. Still, I suggest that decisions are made by motivated people and that others follow.

It's a risky course to generalize. However, my personal observations convince me that people, who make the decisions of the marketplace, still respond very forcefully to profit opportunities. I recognize that the definition of profit that I have chosen is broader perhaps than the economist would like and certainly broader than my traditional technical accounting friends would like. Yet decision makers are not likely to be guided by our definition of profit. They will see profit as a potential advantage to themselves and act to pursue that advantage, whether we understand their perception or not.

Certainly, profit potential changes as circumstances change. Is it not reasonable that the decision maker's perception of profit potential changes and shifts as circumstances change? I have the feeling sometimes that the challenge to profit today is, in fact, a challenge to our traditional understanding of profit. The market, in its wisdom, may have moved on and left us contemplating yesterday's theory. I have an enormous respect for that market and its ability to ferret out profit potential.

I know that the decision makers in the market depend on a great variety of information in their search for an opportunity for profit. As an accountant, I would like to see my profession step up its efforts to understand the decision maker's definition of profit and the sources of information that he uses. The market is merciless, and if the accounting profession is to remain viable, it must recognize a changing market for its services and be ready to meet the market's new needs. Having said that, I would also like to emphasize that there are limits to the capabilities of the accounting system. I would not pretend that accountants can measure and report on profit in the way the market perceives it or I have defined it. We can, however, measure and report on measurable pieces.

The decision makers can then take this core information and add their own perceptions as they evaluate the opportunities for profit potential. Those different perceptions, and the unique information that individual investors ferret out for themselves, make for competition and an effective market. But our profession has to do a better job of giving the investors that core information.

For example, the financial press explained that Wall Street's January bull market was in anticipation of higher reported earnings. The stock market apparently does focus on reported income, not because it represents profit, but because it is one indicator of potential profit. Because I believe profit motivates, and because I believe that the market uses reported net income as an indicator of future profits, I am sensitive to the failure of the accounting profession's present techniques for measuring net income. Perhaps the most significant failing is that our traditional, historic cost-accounting model is unable to deal with the results of inflation. Let me cite a widely quoted statistic from Treasury Secretary Simon. He stated that in 1965, reported earnings of nonfinancial corporations were $38 billion. In 1974, 9 years later, reported earnings were $66 billion—an apparent increase of 74 percent over those earlier results. But, if those 1974 results were adjusted to eliminate inventory profits and to provide for depreciation on a replacement-cost basis, reported results would fall to $21 billion, a decline of 45 percent from 1965. Secretary Simon called this phenomenon "public relations bookkeeping." Reginald Jones criticized the accounting profession's fixation on historic costs when he said, "Business is making wrong decisions on the basis of wrong financial information."

In an attempt to deal with inflation's distorting effect, the SEC has proposed—and I believe seriously intends to require this year—disclosure of some replacement-cost information. Personally, I agree generally with the thrust of the SEC proposal, although I wish it had come from our profession. Inflation must be considered in the reporting of profits, and the SEC's suggested supplementary disclosures are a good first step. Alternatively, the Financial Accounting Standards Board has suggested that financial data be restated in terms of purchasing power. We believe that a purchasing-power restatement would be no more than a mathematical exercise, and a dangerous one at that. The application of a universal index to all companies would imply that all companies are affected by inflation in the same way. I believe that the potential for misleading information in a purchasing-power system might well offset any benefits to be derived.

It is my opinion that we need to use this time, when we are all so cognizant of the effects of inflation, to develop a current-value model. Under current-value accounting, all measurable assets and liabilities would be reported at their fair values at the date of the financial statements. And instead of an income statement, there would be a statement of operations, recognizing current revenues and current costs, and a statement of changes in asset and liability values. The objective of current-value reporting would be to come as close to measuring economic reality as is possible. We know that it can be done because our clients have had some successful experiments. Philips has been doing it for many years in the Netherlands. Barber-Ellis, one of our Canadian clients, issued their financial statements on a current-value basis last year for the first time. Incidentally, Barber-Ellis's reported net income dropped, and their earnings per share dropped by 40 percent. Their effective tax rate was not 47 percent, it was 60 percent.

There has been a lot of talk about using a current-value basis for the preparation of financial statements, and there are some ongoing arguments about what it means. Some argue that current-value accounting should be based on the present value of future cash flows; others argue for current replacement cost; and still others for net realizable value. These are all interesting arguments, but the time for debate is past. Some time ago, my firm took a very strong stand in favor of current-value accounting. We have been trying to encourage discussion of the ideas by sponsoring seminars across the country—and by challenging people to test the ideas in experiments with their own company's data. In the last few months, we have talked to thousands of the leaders in the accounting profession, academe, business, and government. We have been greatly encouraged by what we have heard—the move to current values is gathering momentum.

And finally, my experience with the development of current-value accounting has given me the chance to look at the business of establishing accounting principles in a new light, and I would like to share this insight with you. I have become increasingly concerned about the power wielded in the determination of accounting principles. For example, if purchasing-power-price-level adjusted accounting were adopted, profits would benefit from inflation's effect on long-term debt. Might that basis of accounting encourage extended leverage? Or, as another example, the Financial Accounting Standards Board has, on the basis of principle, determined that research and development costs must be charged to operations immediately, whether or not the research activity seems to be productive. It is too soon to tell I suppose, but I wonder whether that decision will inhibit the financing of longer-term research and development programs. And I have often wondered whether the accountants' preoccupation with earnings per share in the 1960s might have influenced the financial silliness of those years—mergers were often put together with paper, simply to influence the EPS multiple. Did our attention to earnings per share encourage the frantic trading in the market? Or was our attention drawn to the determination of earnings per share because of the market's interest in it as a simplistic measuring stick?

If it is true that profits and earnings motivate the decision makers in the marketplace, then those who determine how earnings are measured have a serious responsibility to the market system. How important it is that accounting principles remain as neutral as possible, avoiding any editorial implications about good or bad activities or any bias toward pressure groups. I have become convinced that accounting principles must be determined in an open environment, dominated in effect by a "market" of their own.

While it is true that the accounting profession, in general, has a responsibility to develop useful, informative accounting principles, I know I must also point at the practitioner individually. It must be said that individually, accountants can be accused of liberally interpreting the principles of measuring earnings, thereby mismotivating decision makers and causing them to misallocate essential resources. The accounting profession *must* be reminded that it has a vital stake in the health of the market system. We, of course, are responsible to our clients and to the investors and potential investors who read our client's reports. But in a larger sense, we are responsible to society as well. If we contribute to the misallocation of this society's resources, we will be (and are) called to task. We must be reminded that our place in this market system is justified only as long as we help make it work. The profession must continually challenge itself to take the long view. You, in business and in the academic community, must also challenge us and help us keep on course.

And so, let me recap. I believe that individual decision makers are motivated to pursue their own personal benefits. And, given a changing world, it is natural that the individual decision maker's perception of personal gain will change. But fundamentally, this thing we call *profit* is no more than an aggregation of individual, personal benefits. Our definition of profit is really irrelevant—it is the individual decision maker's perception of profit potential that moves the market.

In addition, I believe that the role of the accounting profession is to report on that part of "profit" that can be measured. We must challenge the individual practicing accountant to view his daily work in that broad perspective. And as a member of the profession as a whole, I recognize that I must keep the profession moving to develop better measurement tools so that we can meet the decision maker's need for profitability information. Specifically, I am convinced that we must move away from the simplistic, historical, cost-accounting model and begin the development of a more comprehensive, more relevant, current-value system.

Let me make this final observation. I am very pleased that you invited a member of the accounting profession to be a part of this program. Together, as accountants and economists, we have a joint obligation to our society to nurture and protect the market system. That obligation transcends our professional affiliations. That obligation is an opportunity to work *together* to understand this thing called *profit*, to measure it carefully, and to make profitability information realistic and more readily available to the decision makers who make up our market.

4

Profits and Capital Formation in Other Economic Systems

Erik Lundberg

It is indeed a very ambitious title—not selected by myself. I must immediately relieve you of any expectations that I will, or even could, cover and compare a number of other economic systems such as the Yugoslav, Polish, Soviet, and Chinese with that of the United States. I prefer to talk about challenges to the role of profits as they appear in the Scandinavian countries, and especially about attitudes and policies in Sweden.

I do this not only because I like to deal with problems that I know about. The Swedish scene is a good starting point for a discussion of how and why critical attitudes toward the role of profits in a mixed economy of the Swedish type—when being taken seriously in the form of actual policies—will ultimately mean transforming the economy into another type of system. That system will increasingly resemble a socialist one. From this point of view, my lecture may give insight into the position of profits in actual socialist societies. The emphasis will thus be on the difficult transformation process from something rather close to the U.S. capitalist system to something that I have named *fund socialism*.

Why would you be interested in hearing a Swedish economist discuss the changing attitudes toward profits according to socialist thinking in the Scandinavian countries? There are, of course, many possible answers. The three answers that I prefer—and I hope you like—are:

1. That Swedish economists have a tradition of being close to policy issues and political decision making. We are forced to take a stand—or sometimes even to propagate—new, radical ideas.
2. That there is an environment in the Scandinavian countries conducive to the development of more or less radical changes of policy. There is a receptive attitude toward economists' proposals.
3. Swedish policy ideas and attitudes, especially if they are applied, tend to be observed and sometimes taken as a forecast of future attitudes and policies in other countries.

When lecturing in West Germany, for instance, I found the following to be representative of the type of attitude held by German business economists: Sweden's economic development and policy problems as such are not very interesting, Sweden being such an insignificant part of the world. But it may be that tendencies in Swedish social and economic policy—tendencies that we tend to dislike—will be part of our future. The more harmonious the political and social climate among the Scandinavian countries, the more time these countries will have to take up and work out new economic policy experiments. So let us watch them, at least as warning examples.

My intention is to present to you some hot issues from the political debate in Sweden, issues that relate to the role and place of profits in a modern mixed economy. Some that I shall concentrate on are elements of current policy, but more important, imply substantial transformation of the economy.

The attitudes and issues are thus mainly taken from the Swedish scene. But they are very much the same in Denmark and Norway—and there are of course many links with current ideas in, for instance, West Germany and Holland. It is natural that the ideas and attitudes behind policy issues mostly originate from the social democratic parties and the trade unions.

The theme of my lecture is why and how a mixed economy of the Swedish type is being transformed and probably will be transformed quite radically in the near future. The road of transformation leads away from a mixed economy dominated by competitive markets, with private ownership and profits and profit criteria as leading principles, toward some kind of "fund socialism." In this coming system, markets and profits will play a more limited role in the process of development and resource allocation.

It is interesting to study the driving forces or the political-economic motives behind this transformation process against the background of prevalent critical attitudes and ideas about the place of profits in the system. Let me present just the following five critical issues:

1. *Profits and inflation.* High actual or expected profits tend to provoke wage inflation—partly in the form of wage drift. And profits are normally regarded as excess profits somewhere in the economy.
2. *Profits as targets for efficiency.* The competitive pressure in a market economy to attain higher productivity, and thereby increase profits or avoid losses—this "profitability spirit"—is under heavy criticism.
3. *Declining confidence in the profitability criterion.* This has occurred for investment allocation and structural development, not only with regard to neglected external effects. Experiences in recent years of misallocated investments in the production capacity of ships, steel, aeroplanes, motor cars, etc. are taken as evidence of the *failures* of the price and profit formation system, especially under conditions of rapid inflation. There is growing mistrust of the ability of the price system to induce a correct allocation over time of exhaustible raw material resources. For example, high expected profitability of the investments in the Swedish paper and pulp industries tends to lead to bad investment decisions, i.e., overexpansion, given the fact that the wood supply is severely limited. Sufficiently high wood prices are not believed in or accepted as an allocation instrument. It is interesting to contrast this type of inefficiency with the more

systematic inefficiencies of a centrally planned system. Sometimes the planned, stable price system of Eastern socialist countries is even taken as a superior basis for investment planning. In this category belongs a strong mistrust in the functioning of the capital markets—not least the stock exchange—for giving meaningful information as to the cost of capital.

4. *The inequitable effect of profits on income distribution.* This is, of course, a very old issue, but it has attracted rising attention during the last 10 years in the Scandinavian countries. With the acceleration of inflation, the problem of *capital gains* has come to the foreground.

5. *Wealth distribution.* During the last 4 to 5 years, political attention has focused on wealth distribution combined with issues of concentration of ownership and power. From this point of view, profits are a source of accumulation for a small minority of the richest families. There has recently been much political agitation but also serious economic debate about the unequal distribution of wealth, the tendency of profit-savings to create growing inequality, and the power concentration following such inequality.

Certainly these five points of argument about the strategic position of profits are not new to academic or political debate. Criticism of profits is not based, as Professor Harris suggested yesterday, on incorrect information about actual profit and wealth statistics. New policies are being drawn up and carried out as practical solutions to perceived deficiencies. Before I discuss these policies, let me mention the somewhat paradoxical background to the radical changes in social democratic and trade union attitudes toward the role of profits.

Changing Attitudes toward the Role of Profits

It is important to stress that criticism of the market and profit system in Sweden, and the strong political will to change it, has arisen despite its apparent great success during the whole postwar period, including the 1970s. All the usual performance criteria point in the direction of success: full employment has been the rule during the whole period, with a 1 to 2 percent unemployment rate. Even in the present recession, the rate has not surpassed the 2 percent level. The growth record has been relatively good—4.5 percent annual growth of real GNP up to 1970 and around 3 percent in the 1970s. Starting from a relatively high level at the end of the war, this development has brought Swedish per capita GNP to an unparalleled world position. Inflation has not been worse than in the average OECD country. The rapid expansion of the public sector has, according to certain measures, made its share the largest of all Western countries. Social needs seem to be less neglected than in most other countries. The extreme progressivity of the income tax plus a successful aiding of low-income groups, especially during the last 10 years, has brought about a significant equalization of income distribution after taxes.

But as Schumpeter once remarked, success can be more efficient in bringing about discontent than failure. And as he stressed, it is very much the intellectuals, the academics in the socialist party, and the trade union movement who lead the way and provoke new attitudes. Schumpeter showed how the *rational attitude* easily tends to attack private property—that the criticism of the capitalist order proceeds from a critical attitude of mind.

Capitalism inevitably creates, educates and subsidizes a vested interest in social unrest. And the capitalist order cannot control its intellectual sector effectively— the intellectual group cannot help nibbling because it lives on criticism—and more important it often carries a *moral disapproval* of private property and the capitalist order.

Schumpeter said this in the early forties (in *Capitalism, Socialism and Democracy*). But his ideas can easily be applied to the Swedish scene of today. For such intellectual criticism to have an impact on society, the rank and file must be willing to listen, powerful, and aware of the urgency of the message. These conditions are reasonably well satisfied in Sweden.

To this should be added the fact that Sweden has in large part avoided the economic problems currently plaguing other industrial nations. Having reached a rather affluent position at which satisfaction of the usual aim is taken for granted, Sweden can now afford to create new problems by elevating the aspiration level and experimenting with the system.

The radical change during the last two decades in the attitudes of leading socialist and trade union leaders toward the place of profits gives a good illustration. One important cause of the rapid rise in productivity in Swedish industry during the fifties and sixties—by 7 to 8 percent per year—was the strong shift of resources—labor and capital—from less to more productive activities among regions, branches, and plants. High mobility of labor was supported to an increasing extent by accommodating labor-market policies. And the guidance of profits and profitability criteria in this process was generally accepted.

One can find remarkable assertions made by leading trade union people in the 1950s demonstrating great confidence in the working of the profit system undisturbed by selective government interference. The support took the following form when the textile and clothing industries were hit by a structural crisis and the question of protection came up. A chairman of the textile union said something like this:

We prefer working in profitable branches and firms to getting protection from the Government. Our employers want protection but we disagree. If firms become unprofitable and employment opportunities weaken, then we are prepared to move to profitable and expanding activities—that must exist in a full employment economy as guaranteed by the Government's general policies.

It was a liberal attitude, based on the insight that as a small country Sweden's prosperity depended fundamentally on foreign trade—on the competitiveness of Swedish industry. The trade union attitude toward profitability, productivity, and flexibility can be contrasted to the corresponding British attitudes and reactions of the time. And the actual result was a remarkably smooth transfer of employment from textile and clothing to engineering, with significant contributions to total productivity.

Since the end of the sixties, the outlook has changed radically. In the language of welfare analysis, the benefits of rising productivity have been heavily counterbalanced by the social costs of high mobility in the form of layoffs of older and professionally handicapped people, more frequent periods of unemployment, regional imbalances, etc. This view implies that the applied profit criteria are misleading. They do not contain all necessary information. The successful policy of the fifties and sixties is presently regarded as a partial or even total failure. The present policies decree heavy constraints on labor mobility and new ambitions as to full employment. It is not only the local employment that has to be protected, demands for security of employment within plants have become strong and have been supported by new legislation tending to make labor more of a fixed cost.

All this implies dethronement of profitability as a criterion for the allocation of resources. The government should and does to an increasing extent interfere with results dictated by the price and profit mechanisms. This type of activity is more or less typical for most Western countries, although the shift in attitude and policies may have been more drastic in the Scandinavian countries than elsewhere. Policy targets other than growth and stability, such as security of employment, regional, environmental, and distributional goals, have become so important that the profit criterion is much less reliable as a guide.

There is another reaction to the successful combination of growth and full employment policies during the fifties and sixties. That reaction has much to do with the conception of how profits are created and the key role they seem to play in the growth process. In the back of the minds of trade union economists there is a kind of primitive Salter model. The idea is that in each branch of industry there is a fringe of firms or plants with old and obsolete machinery and relatively low productivity. A rather successful application of uniform wage policy implying equal pay for equal work, independent of productivity and profitability of the individual plant, means that high or "surplus" profits of intramarginal firms and plants are not expropriated by wage increases. It is asserted that the trade unions hold back demands that could be satisfied in the most profitable firms of each branch. The wage increases are instead mainly determined by the productivity of the marginal firms, because of a desire to preserve employment. According to this model, then, there will be an element of surplus, unexploited profits having the character of rent for the intramarginal, high-productivity firms. From this point of view, these profits have the character of untapped wage-payment capacity. There is no need to apply Marxian "Mehrwert" theory and exploitation concepts. These surplus or excess profits after tax and divided payments will be plowed back into capital formation and in this way build up the fortunes of the rich. This wealth-distribution argument has been taken very seriously during recent years. It is easy to demonstrate how strongly concentrated stock ownership is—1 percent owning 70 percent—and how the self-financing process will tend to preserve or aggravate these inequalities. It is in fact easier to provoke "statistical indignation" with regard to wealth than with regard to income distribution.

The Swedish tradition of liberal taxation of capital gains and corporate profits with generous allowances for depreciation of machinery and inventories surfaces frequently in arguments on the distribution issue. The matter is complicated, however, because owners of private wealth do not get much income after all taxes are accounted for. The very high taxes on personal capital income added to a yearly wealth tax mean that the marginal tax on returns for wealthy people is usually above 100 percent. In addition, the internal rate of return on shares during the last 10 years, even before taxes, including the average rise in share prices, has just equalled the rate of inflation. The real return after tax has been negative. Thus share prices have not kept pace with the net accumulation of capital within corporations. But this fact has had little impact on the attitudes of critics of the profit system.

Capital formation out of profits also leads to criticism of the functioning of the capital market. The high degree of self-financing suggests an imperfection in the market for risk capital. This self-financed part of risk capital might have too low an imputed capital cost, causing misallocation of resources. Putting some of these funds on the capital market should, other things being equal, make it a little less imperfect.

Policy Suggestions

Let me now discuss some policy suggestions arising from this socialist account of sins and malfunctioning of the profit system. Observe that I only consider actual policies or serious policy proposals—not irresponsible leftist views. There are three alternative policy strategies:

1. To find methods *to squeeze the average profit margins.*
2. *To find ways of profit sharing,* thereby eventually creating tolerance for reasonably high profitability.
3. To find far-reaching schemes for *collectivization (or socialization) of savings,* which imply a shift of ownership and control of economic power. Efficient plans of this type would ultimately lead to a radical change in the politicoeconomic system.

The profit-squeeze approach is based on the idea that profits are partially rent. If wage costs can be shifted upward (e.g., by means of rising wage taxes) above the limits dictated by employment protection in marginal firms, the share of profits can be reduced. Full employment can be maintained in spite of this by various kinds of subsidies to plants with marginal employment. This type of policy should also dampen the wage drift arising from surplus profits in intramarginal plants.

In a way, this policy strategy has been applied in Sweden since the beginning of the 1960s. The introduction of pension reform was combined with rising contributions from the total wage bill into a collective pension fund under control of the government. This fund has now reached the size of one third of the GNP; translated to U.S. conditions, this corresponds to about $600 billion.

The yearly growth of this collective fund has recently been about equal to the whole of household savings. The trade union theory was that part of this fund saving should result from squeezing profits. And we have actually observed a considerable amount of squeezing of profit margins in Swedish industry and a significant decline of average profitability during the sixties. The trouble is, however, that this is a world phenomenon, a trend of declining profitability having occurred in nearly all Western capitalist countries starting at different times in the sixties. There are many interpretations of this phenomenon that I have not time to deal with here. Anyhow, the decline of profitability in industry has at the given rate of investment implied a simultaneous decline in the solvency of corporations. Compared to British and American corporations, the profitability of even leading Swedish companies seems remarkably low. One consequence is that the ratio of debt to equity in Swedish corporations might be 3 to 1 on the average.

The trade union reaction to the big rise of profit margins and profitability in 1973-1974 was very strong. There appeared wild accusations of excess profits. Inflation and strong leverage effects implied a very big rise in the profitability of holding equity. Although the profitability in real terms—correcting for the higher rate of inflation in those years—was just on a par with the good years in the sixties, the criticism was severe and resulted, with a lag, in explosive wage and salary increases. The negative reaction to high profits and concentrated ownership from the side of leading social democrats and trade union leaders has for these various reasons become very strong. There was a short-term neutralization of the "excess profits" in 1974, brought about in a typical Swedish compromise by a government decree putting a considerable share of the profits accrued into existing special funds to be used for financing investment in environmental improvements.

There is a serious dilemma caused by this political intolerance of even reasonably high profits. The rate of net profits after taxes and dividends should, according to reasonable norms, correspond to the rate of the growth of total capital. This "golden rule" implies that the solvency of corporations ought not to be reduced any further. Since new corporate equity issues are small in relation to existing equity capital, this rule mandates a level of nominal profits that seems quite high. According to present 5-year plans, Swedish industry and trade should expand by about 7 percent in volume, capital expanding at about the same rate. Given an inflation rate of 7 to 8 percent, the after-tax rate of profit should amount to about 15 percent, on average perhaps 50 percent higher than at present. Such raising of average profits, brought about by a combination of devaluation and restrictive wage policy, would, according to the trade union view, result in an intolerable rise in share prices and fortunes of the rich.

Various systems of profit sharing are intensively discussed against this background. It should be mentioned that the trade union economists in West Germany are pioneers in this field. The tremendous accumulation of private wealth due to the rapid growth of the German economy has provoked the issues of *Vermogenspolitik*. The Swedes have learned a lot from the lively German debate, but are closer to political solutions. It is interesting to note that in contrast to the Germans, Swedish trade unionists generally oppose solutions on an individual basis, where employees' individual ownership would grow successively in individual firms and be supported by government subsidies. There are three main arguments made against such solutions: (1) individual wage—and salary—earners have no great desire to own shares—according to experience, the majority will sell the shares quickly to buy durable goods and houses; (2) the solidarity of workers in the unions and in the total collective of unions might be endangered if ownership of firms created new loyalties and attachments; and (3) such schemes would tend to create new inequalities between those employed in good and bad firms, and in this way break the solidarity of the masses of trade union members. The egalitarian spirit is very strong.

There is a strong fear among leading trade union people of creating a bourgeois spirit and capitalist mentality in the common worker, who would perhaps learn to love his small fortune in shares as well as the firm where he is employed. We may find an analogy in Mao's Chinese agricultural policy: more than 10 percent private ownership is dangerous—passing that threshold means the appearance of egotism and disruptive competitive forces in the community. In fact, there is not much belief in the positive incentive and productivity effects of individual profit-sharing systems.

The system of profit and capital sharing recently proposed by the central trade union organization is based on obligatory shares of net profits of 20 percent. The union funds created and accumulated from these profit shares will be used for direct reinvestment into stocks of the same company. There will be only collective ownership. In this way, the participation by employees in the formation of risk capital should, according to the trade union economists, mean "minimum disturbance" to the present market system. Profits and profitability should be working as incentives in an unchanged way and function as a source of financing as before, plowed back by means of direct issues to the wage funds; managements do not care where the money comes from. Ownership of corporations should in this way gradually be shifted over to the employees, or the bureaucracies of the funds. There are lots of complications on all levels of such a scheme. Models have been worked out to show the speed of transfer of ownership to the wage funds. The predominant answer is that within 10 to 25 years, the employees' representatives will have majority or leading positions among shareholders and on the boards of all companies with more than 50 employees.

Hopes and Fears

Can this transformation proceed in a frictionless way? And how will a fund-socialist economy function? Can we learn something from Eastern socialist systems, perhaps especially from the Yugoslav model with worker-owned enterprises? The Swedish debate is full of hopes and fears in the analysis of possible outcomes.

Let me start with the fears—these shed a more interesting light on the Swedish move toward socialism than the hopes. I am sure you can guess whose hopes and fears I am referring to. An obligatory 20 percent or so taken out of net profits, transferred to the wage funds, and plowed back as equity capital will have a strong negative effect on share prices. One can use different models to analyze how stock prices will be affected by a permanent "tax" of this kind. There will first be a one-time effect of lowered share prices (on the order of 20 percent under the simplest conditions). The dilution of the stock of shares by direct issuances, plus the pessimistic anticipation of old share-owners with regard to future dividend policies, might very likely cause a cumulative decline in share prices. That would eventually mean the collapse of the stock exchange and the abolition of private shareholders as important sources of risk capital. In a way this result would imply the end of corporation profits as a source of private savings and shares as part of private property. And the aim of collective ownership of the corporate sector could thus be reached in an "elegant" way without a costly and complicated socialization procedure! The Scandinavian countries have had a tradition of not socializing private industry.

The share-distribution problem having been "solved," the level of corporation profits could be raised without inhibition in order to satisfy the need for an increased supply of savings and risk capital. This is, of course, the method used in socialist countries: by means of price policy, high gross profits can be generated to finance capital formation without anybody getting rich. My feeling is that the malfunctioning of the stock exchange and the deficient supply of risk capital during a transfer period will necessitate supply from new sources. The simplest way—as in the Danish socialist proposal formed a few years ago—is to put a 1 or 2 percent "savings tax fee" on the total wage sum, to be paid into central funds for the supply of risk capital. In this way, the Danes showed, majority ownership of shares could be attained without collapse of the stock market much more rapidly than by means of profit sharing, the sum of wage and salary payments being about 25 times the size of the corporations' net profits. In fact, we in Sweden have slowly started on this route. As part of the big pension fund, a special AP fund is separated for buying shares and also taking care of new issues directed to the fund. This was recently the case with Volvo.

I shall not enter into details and technicalities surrounding these schemes. There are lots of complications, not least with regard to the multinational corporations and small family firms. The political debate and the decision process will be long. The proposal of a profit-sharing system is now a subject of research of a government commission taking its time. Swedes are good at finding workable compromises. I have hopes that there will be no collapse of the present mixed system and no revolution. But the tendencies leading away from a system with private ownership and profits at the center of the economy are clear and strong.

Let me summarize the issues and give some of my own doubts. This will be done against the background of experiences in real socialist systems. The criticism of the present system of profits and ownership in the first place refers to power concentration, based on inequality of the distribution of wealth. The most fundamental change now going on concerns the ownership and management of private corporations. Labor represents around 70 to 75 percent of value added in an average industrial firm, capital only 25 percent. It is not only capital that takes a risk. Shareowners can often shift out of a risky corporation more easily than employees when bad times appear.

Strong reactions from the side of trade unions have appeared against merger decisions often made by a few strong shareholder groups in the companies without concern for the employees. The conclusion is that the employees should share in the decision process and in the responsibilities of firm management on all levels. This means representation of workers on the boards of directors—this is already the case in Sweden as in many other countries. According to new legislation concerning the rights of labor, collective bargaining may and will contain agreements on labor participation in all kinds of decision making, not only organization of work on the factory floor and environment and employment policy but also investment, sales, and merger policies. Thus a considerable part of the power problem can be solved without a radical change in ownership. Ownership through wage funds will complement the new labor rights by encouraging interest and responsibility for the development of the corporation, and ultimately implying a majority position on boards. Anybody can imagine the danger that drawn out, bureaucratic decision processes can pose to the functioning of a corporation. There is already a lot of it. A new type of manager and management personnel will be needed to take care of and have patience with the new type of bargaining characteristic of these decision processes.

On the positive side is the possible mobilization of knowledge and skill from much broader layers than at present. The negative side has to do with bureaucratization, slowing up of important decisions, risks of higher frequency of strikes, and consequent lower efficiency.

And what will happen to profits as a criterion of efficiency and guide for resource allocation? My guess is that the role of profits and profitability will be challenged and reduced, both as criteria of efficiency with regard to use of resources and as sources of financing. Wage costs will probably continue to squeeze profit margins in big sectors of private industry as well as in marginal firms. The stronger place of labor in the firms will strengthen the goals of keeping up employment. The talents of new management groups will partly be used for persuading the government to support and finance or take over weak branches and firms. The central government will be involved to an increasing extent in private business—the mixed economy will be more mixed. There will be a greater politization of entrepreneurial decision making.

In Sweden we have the new and rather dramatic spectacle of private industry offering steel plants, shipyards, and textile plants to the government to be taken over completely or as joint ventures. Profitability is expected to continue to be very low—there are losses at present—and in a situation aggravated by excess capacity, competition with socialized industries in other countries is often deemed hopeless. But I do not take this as an indication of a loss of vitality in private industry. On the contrary, private business will use the released capital for new investment in more profitable branches.

On the other hand, in corporations with relatively good prospects and high profitability, the profit-sharing device and the policies of the wage-fund boards will generate as yet unknown criteria for expansion and efficiency. Certain problems of the Yugoslav system might appear. With decentralized wage funds (on the firm level) and trade union dominated entrepreneurship, there will be the desire to maximize value added per employee and to preserve existing employment. Such tendencies can be anticipated and counteracted by means of more integrated wage funds (on branch levels) and government policy interference. Employment priorities of the firm or of the region at the cost of profitability tests may result in the development of "conspicuous production," i.e., investments in big ostentatious projects at a relatively low expected profitability. After a transition period with high capital costs, the wage and AP funds might set—in the absence of rigorous market tests—a low target rate of profitability.

All this would mean a more suboptimal allocation of resources needed for expansion, which would be unobservable *ex post*. On the other hand, profit criteria can and probably will still be effectively applied with regard to short-term efficiency when considering, for example, rationalization investment or substitution of machinery for labor. Internal rates of 30 percent can be used in rating such projects without effects on distribution. It could be added that the reforms of the economic systems in Eastern socialist countries seem to imply the use of profitability criteria just for efficiency control, but not for choice of long-term investment projects. The analogy is dangerous, however. The information content of prices on which the profitability calculations are based in an open economy will be of very different value in Sweden under fund socialism than in Poland or East Germany.

I have pictured a clear trend in Sweden toward a form of socialism including a more modest role for profits than at present. Without doubt, the same tendencies exist in other European countries, but in most respects are perhaps less pressing than in Sweden. There are some similarities with the socialist systems in Eastern Europe. But I warn against easy analogies and belief in convergence theories. Let me mention some of the checks and balances, the countervailing powers, slowing up the socialization process in a Western country like Sweden.

Sweden is a small, very open country—strongly dependent on foreign trade and capital movements. We undertake serious risks by moving too rapidly ahead of other Western European countries on the road to socialism. And this is clearly understood by our social democratic government. The international price and market system will continue to determine profitability and resource allocation in strategic sectors of the economy. The multinational corporations, responsible for 60 percent of industrial investment and 75 percent of exports, must be allowed to operate on a competitive basis, which means a lot of disturbing compromises within a collective wage-fund scheme.

The place of the consumers tends to be forgotten in this type of discussion. The cooperative movement in Sweden is strong, both economically and politically. Our industries and shops work in the market system, looking for profits, profitable investments, and lines of development. But the surplus ultimately takes the form of low prices and rebates to their consumer members, who are mostly from the same group of people that makes up the trade unions. From this it follows that the cooperative socialists are not enthusiastic about wage-fund systems and trade union dominance of management. And generally it must be maintained that employment is not an end in itself but a means to satisfy the needs of the consumers. Profits in a market system are generally better guides for covering the consumers' demands than the short-term, often arbitrary criteria that will be used by trade union dominated boards.

Also to be considered are the small family firms, great in number but with a limited share of total employment. Inheritance and fortune taxes plus all kinds of other government charges have meant serious difficulties and a decreased survival probability for them. The owners and their employees play a political role, and their situation does not easily fit into fund socialism.

My conclusion is that the strength of a mixed economic system of the Swedish type is its pluralistic nature. There will always be strong reactions to new kinds of power concentration, from private-property owners, the central government, or the trade union organizations. The road to "fund socialism" will mean serious limitations in the power arising from profits and private ownership. But the emergence of socialism will be long and drawn out, with lots of compromises along the way and rather unknown results.

Commentary

Abram Bergson

The theme of this symposium is profits, and Professor Lundberg has focused on that topic in the context of the Swedish experience. Rather than comment expressly on his very illuminating exposition, I propose to consider profits very briefly in another context with which I am more familiar. I refer to socialism of the thoroughgoing sort where there is predominant, if not universal, public ownership of the means of production.

As is well known, such socialism theoretically might be organized variously, but in practice use has been made again and again of one form of organization in particular. I refer to the scheme that has come to be known as "centralist planning": essentially, production units to a great extent are coordinated and directed by superior agencies in bureaucratic structures and through the use of extramarket devices, such as physical quotas. Why centralist planning has turned out to be predominant is an interesting question that I cannot pursue here. But so far as it has, our attention inevitably turns especially to that scheme. Of particular interest, too, is the experience under it in the U.S.S.R., the country where centralist planning originated, where it has accordingly had most time to mature, and where its operation by now has also been studied in some depth.

While the U.S.S.R. has largely dispensed with private enterprise and markets as we know them, certain institutions characterizing the Western mixed economy are still very much present there. I refer particularly to money, prices, and financial accounting. Indeed, it is evidently only because of the persistence of those features that there is in the U.S.S.R. any such thing as profits for us to discuss at all. The persistence of those features and the persistence of profits along with them, nevertheless, still sometimes occasion surprise, but they are hardly novelties. Some Soviet theoreticians, it is true, once urged their abolition, and at one time they were nearly abolished in fact, but that was long ago. Ever since then, money, prices, financial accounting, and profits have been established features in the U.S.S.R., and ones rarely, if ever, challenged.

That profits have survived in the U.S.S.R. in that way already tells us something of their role in economic life there. Like profits in the Western mixed economy, they are necessarily integral to financial controls over the activities of economic entities. Under Soviet centralist planning, such controls are no less needed than they are in the West. But the question arises as to what the role of profits may be in Soviet economic life more generally. We also wish to know how, if at all, the Russians perform under centralist-planning economic functions such as are rewarded by profits in Western mixed economies.

These, however, are very large questions. I shall focus here on but one aspect, though a cardinal one. As Schumpeter taught us long ago, among the different activities rewarded by profits in the West, not least is that of entrepreneurship. Entrepreneurship, moreover, is seen essentially as the initial introduction and diffusion of productive technologies and products of the novel sort that we usually call *innovations*. It seems fitting to consider here, if only in the most summary way, the Soviet experience in this sphere.

Regarding that experience, a usual supposition today, I think, is that Soviet centralist planning has been shown to be unimpressive in innovation. I may as well say at once that I have no quarrel at all to pick with that view. On the contrary, all that I know only seems to confirm it. It may be instructive nevertheless to probe a bit further into the question at issue. To begin with, if Soviet centralist planning has indeed been unimpressive with respect to innovation, what is the reason?

The answer, I think, is essentially a very simple and familiar one: bureaucracy. Of course, bureaucracy is not exactly unknown in the West either, and up to a point it obviously must have its rationale economically. Under Soviet centralist planning, however, there are reasons to think that bureaucracy often goes beyond that point. That is so with respect to economic affairs generally; it seems especially so with respect to innovation.

The resulting difficulties are a familiar subject of complaint in the U.S.S.R. itself. To refer only to some of the more outstanding ones, there is the need to keep account and to calculate in terms of the proverbially dubious, administered ruble prices, which only compounds the risks already inherent in innovation in any event; the notable multiplicity of agencies often concerned with any project, and the correspondingly complex task of coordination thus encountered; the related difficulties of integrating into the economy a novel vector of productive inputs and outputs, where such productive inputs and outputs are often rationed rather than being available in markets; and last but not least, the apparently weak incentives often offered for overcoming such hurdles. This calls for further comment.

In the U.S.S.R., in the sixth decade since the October Revolution, egalitarianism in income distribution is still an avowed goal, but no one supposes that it is a fact. On the contrary, incomes continue to be, as they long have been, systematically differentiated to reflect skill levels and the nature of the task. That is true of workers generally and so also of scientific workers and managerial personnel in economic organizations. In short, circumstances affecting incentives would seem, on the face of it, to favor rather than inhibit innovation. On closer scrutiny, however, they turn out to be otherwise.

True, people responsible for useful inventions might be granted a special reward for their achievement. Though of a modest one-time sort, such a reward has no doubt been to the good. True too, and from the present standpoint much more important, managerial personnel in the economy, depending on their performance, customarily receive not only basic salaries but bonuses. Determined under intricate schemes that almost defy summary, however, the chief of such bonuses depends first and foremost on performance in fulfilling more or less general plan targets, such as those for sales, profits, and the like. Should an innovation favor that result, that would be to the good and the bonuses for overall performance might be somewhat larger than they would be otherwise. Special bonuses might be earned also for the innovation itself. But here too, rewards have tended to be of a relatively modest once-for-all kind. Should disruption attendant on the innovation impair fulfillment of more general targets, there might be no gain to speak of. Disconcertingly, an innovation, if successful, might also result in the imposition of unduly taxing plan targets in future.

Not too surprisingly, therefore, managerial personnel seem again and again to prefer the quiet life to innovation, so, at any rate, we are led to infer from ever-recurring Soviet complaints—complaints such as the one by Z. Sirotkin, Chief Design Engineer, Bielorussian Motor Vehicle Plant, and U.S.S.R. State Laureate (as quoted in Berliner's new study on Soviet innovation):

Unfortunately the "mechanism" of the Economic Reform has proved insufficiently effective when applied to the question of putting new equipment into production. After all, the manufacture of a new machine means, first of all, new concerns and difficulties. The work rhythm is disrupted, and many new problems appear. Under the existing situation, this causes the performance indicators to decline and the enterprise incentive funds to grow smaller. It is for this reason that some plant executives brush aside innovations proposed by science. . . . This is especially true if the plant has achieved a stable work rhythm and high quality output and has all the benefits the Economic Reform provides; as for material incentives to induce changes, there are none.

In a time of general well-being the plant manager would have to be a very far-seeing person indeed to feel any concern or anxiety, and to undertake the preparatory work for producing a new model of the machine. For in the next few years that promises many difficulties.

I have been referring especially to the system of rewards for managerial personnel in the "enterprise" (*predpriiatie*), the agency traditionally in charge of a production unit. At all levels of the economic bureaucracies, successful innovation can be favorable to a managerial career; but here too what apparently counts above all is performance with respect to more general plan indicators.

My concern is with Soviet centralist planning; but if under that system incentives to innovate have their limitations, that must also be true of the corresponding rewards that are familiar in the West. Nevertheless, one wonders whether the latter can be so ineffective so often. More generally, with all its shortcomings as a mechanism to generate innovation, Soviet centralist planning must be accounted as also having some virtues. Most important, while the inventor is rewarded, he receives no restrictive entitlement whatever to his invention, so limitations on use such as are possible under Western patents are quite avoided. Commercial secrecy also cannot be at all consequential.

Granting that, it seems difficult to avoid concluding, at least in respect of innovation, that Soviet centralist planning must often be at a disadvantage compared with the mixed economies that we know in the West. If it is, it should be observed; that would help explain an outstanding feature of the Soviet growth process that is otherwise difficult to understand.

I refer to the fact that over a protracted post-World War II period, the U.S.S.R., with respect to the rate of growth of output per worker, has been unable to more than match Western countries at comparable economic levels. It has been unable to do so despite the fact that in the U.S.S.R. the capital stock per worker has grown at extraordinarily rapid rates. Under the circumstances, the U.S.S.R. might have been expected to outpace markedly rather than merely match the West with respect to the growth of output per worker. Among Western countries, only in Japan has the capital stock per worker grown at tempos similar to those in the U.S.S.R. But Japanese output per worker has grown by 8.8 percent yearly, more than twice the corresponding tempo (4.2 percent) in the U.S.S.R. Since one need not be too initiated into problems of productivity measurement to be aware, results such as these may be construed variously. However, there is, I think, at least a presumption that innovation in the U.S.S.R. is not contributing to the growth of output at nearly the rates that Western experience might indicate.

[Even if the Soviet performance has been substandard in the way indicated, it should be observed that Soviet centralist planning cannot be considered as solely at fault. Thus innovation in the U.S.S.R. undoubtedly has suffered also from the quasi-isolation from the West into which the Soviet economy was plunged by the autarkic policies of the early 5-year plans, an isolation that was for a time only reinforced by Western strategic controls, and an isolation from which the U.S.S.R., despite all the attendant fanfare, has still only partially emerged. The U.S.S.R. even so has always sought assiduously to follow Western technological developments, but the adaptation of those developments to Soviet circumstances and their introduction into the U.S.S.R. must often have been impeded nevertheless. True, the quasi-isolation has itself been fostered in a degree, in well-known ways, by Soviet centralist planning, but it has also reflected the government's more basic development policies, and the deleterious effect on innovation must be read in that light.

In addition to the Soviet economic quasi-isolation, it is sometimes suggested that innovation in the U.S.S.R. has also suffered because of the preoccupation there with military research and development. At least, civilian innovation, it is held, must have suffered simply because of the resultant diversion of scarce scientific talents and resources to military work. That could well be so; and so far as it is, Soviet performance in respect of productivity growth would have suffered the more since the available data probably reflect only very imperfectly innovation in final products, whether civilian or military. But it should be observed too that Soviet outlays for research and development have been notably large and, even after due allowance for allocations to military-related activities, probably still compare favorably with corresponding outlays in Western countries at similar economic levels. Moreover, the military research and development must have had some favorable civilian spillovers.]

I referred to the bonuses paid innovative managerial personnel in the Soviet enterprise. These rewards are probably the nearest counterpart in the U.S.S.R. to the entrepreneurial profits on which Schumpeter focused. Moreover, the bonuses are in fact financed in good part, though not entirely, by appropriations from the accounting category "profits" to which I referred at the outset. To what extent, however, the economic gain from innovation is actually captured in the profits of the responsible enterprise is an interesting question. Given the oddities of ruble prices, it is also one not easily answered. In any event, profits from whatever source are for the most part transferred to the government budget rather than retained within the enterprise; as for the amounts retained, those sums are used principally to finance inventories and small-scale fixed investments, diverse "social-cultural" measures, and bonuses such as have been described.

In the great debate over the economic merit of socialism that was waged in the interwar years, a principal issue considered was that concerning comparative performance with respect to innovation under that system. Thus, in Oskar Lange's famous economic case for socialism, a cardinal contention is that that system would provide a solution to the problem posed by the asserted tendency of "monopoly, restrictionism, and interventionism" to limit introduction of new technologies under capitalism. On the other hand, critics such as Hayek, while not seeking to rebut the proponents too explicitly on the question at issue, have obviously been of a different view. Apparently, innovations were expected to be hindered under socialism by the difficulties encountered by overburdened superior agencies in planning new investments and by the probably unavoidable general aversion to risks of managers.

If the Soviet experience is at all indicative, one wonders whether the critics have not been nearer the mark than the proponents. True, the U.S.S.R. has been able to avoid some restrictive arrangements, particularly patents, which Lange stressed as impeding innovation under capitalism. On the other hand, bureaucratic difficulties such as the critics adumbrated have obviously taken a considerable toll under socialism.

Among those difficulties, however, the critics, as indicated, often focused on an asserted managerial reluctance to take risks. If only for clarity, it should be observed that for risky projects such as are in question, theory seemingly prescribes only that socialist managerial personnel, while seeking to maximize their own utilities, must be induced also to heed expected economic returns, whatever those returns may be. With appropriate rewards for success, there is, I believe, no bar in principle to approaching that desideratum. There is no bar to that even if managers should be risk averse, as they apparently are in the U.S.S.R. But for managerial personnel who are risk averse and whose careers as well as earnings depend on success, the rewards might have to be large. That might be so even though losses of capital almost inevitably have to be borne by the community generally.

The Soviet government, we are led to infer, has not found it expedient to allow managerial rewards of the required magnitude. It has not found it expedient to do so very possibly for ideological reasons, although such scruples manifestly have not generally been overpowering. But if managerial personnel have been induced to stress plan fulfillment generally over innovation, that cannot be entirely accidental. Rather, given the difficulties that innovation poses for planning, the government must hesitate on that account too to offer large rewards for innovation.

The working arrangements for innovation under Soviet centralist planning are surely open to improvement, but the deficiencies often seem deep-seated. Moreover, one suspects that the government will continue for some time to have reasons to stress plan fulfillment generally in comparison to innovation. Whether on that account or for ideological reasons, so long as managerial rewards for innovation also remain relatively restricted, it seems permissible to doubt that Soviet performance in that sphere can be nearly such as proponents of socialism seemed to expect.

Commentary

Guido Carli

My purpose today is to present to you some aspects of the transformation of the economic system in my own country, Italy. In recent years in Italy, profits have shown a stronger downward trend than in other industrialized countries. The causes of this phenomenon are interpreted in different ways by employers, workers, and economists. Employers feel that one main cause is that wages have increased more rapidly than productivity. In addition, according to the employer's interpretation, since the economy is an open one, this evolution has had differing impact in nonprotected and protected sectors. The sectors more exposed to foreign competition have suffered most. In the view of workers, the main cause of the downward trend of profits in Italy is poor management and lack of innovation. They compare their wages to the wages in the rest of Europe in the same sectors of industry. Why should wages in the steel industry or the mechanical industry be higher in Germany than in Italy? After all, the level of technological progress is more or less the same.

In the view of economists, the downward trend of profits is in part due to an increase in the cost of social services; the cost of public health is higher in Italy than in the rest of the industrialized world. In addition, industries have been forced to shoulder the costs of inefficiency. Among these costs are the restrictions which have proliferated in recent years with respect to the mobility of labor among and within firms. The monetary policy followed in this period has also played a role.

If we observe the dynamic effect of wage increases on prices in the last decade, we note at first a redistribution of income to the advantage of labor. This is followed by an increase in prices and profits, but never has the increase in prices fully overtaken the increase in labor income gained through labor disputes. In order to protect themselves against price movements, workers in recent years have sought and obtained wage increases as rapidly as possible.

Whatever the explanation of the phenomenon, in Italy as well as in other industrialized nations, corporate profits have shown a constant downward trend. What are the consequences for the Italian economy? Earlier, Henry Wallich described the sequence in the following terms. If we lower profits, firms will seek new sources of external financing. But, he concluded, where there is not enough profit in the entire economy, there will not be much money available to lend. Let me try to describe the evolution of the Italian economy, in which there is not much money available to finance debt. If the financing of new investments by corporations suddenly requires a higher percentage of external capital, the shift favors public enterprises over privately owned enterprises. Second, large enterprises and large corporations have easier access to credit than smaller corporations. As a result, there is a tendency for small enterprises to be absorbed by large enterprises and for private enterprises to be absorbed by the public sector.

There is another aspect on which attention should also be focused. Whatever the type of enterprise, public or private, the recourse to external indebtedness has increased to such an extent that in certain cases it represents 90 percent of the assets owned by the enterprise. The system is threatened by the absence of responsibility. Who is responsible? Shareholders? This is a problem which has not been solved in my country but must be sooner or later. The problem is to assign somebody the responsibilities of conducting the enterprise in accordance with the indications given by the market.

The level of indebtedness makes the productive system more dependent on the behavior of the banking system. In that respect, the allocative function of the banking system is increased. At the same time, the impulses of the monetary policy may be concentrated in a particular segment of the economy. If the public sector is large and if its credit needs are rigid, the full effect is concentrated on the most productive sectors of the economy—the nonprotected sectors, those more exposed to foreign competition. The system reacts more rapidly in the sense of an increase in exports or substitution for imports. But in the end, equilibrium is found at the expense of the level of employment.

What kind of evolution will the future bring to the Italian economic system, given that Italy's Communist party is the strongest one in the Western world? I believe the communists favor integration of the Italian economy in the European economic community. In fact, they favor an acceleration of the process of integration. They accept that we must preserve a section of market economy with a structure similar to that of the rest of the community. To that end, profit is being rediscovered as an institution which helps to allocate resources and stimulate innovation.

In this respect, it is not paradoxical to assert that to a certain extent the Italian Communist party follows not Karl Marx but Adam Smith. I have here some remarks of Adam Smith on profits. Let me start by considering wages and the position of wage earners. What was the view of Adam Smith? Merchants and manufacturers complained much about the bad effects of high wages in raising the price and thereby lessening the sale of their goods both at home and abroad. They said nothing of the bad effects of high profits; they were silent with regard to the pernicious effects of their own gains; they complained only of those of other people. I believe that these views are probably shared in my country by the Communist party, and must add that they are shared by people who are not communist. To quote from *The Wealth of Nations*, "Men do not by nature prefer the active and energetic life to the life of indolence and repose." Smith feared that the rise in the rate of profits would reduce the quality if not the supply of capital's effort. This might be the consensus in my own country. The future evolution may therefore be in the direction which has been followed in

Sweden, toward restoration of a certain area of a market economy on the conviction that the market economy better manages the use of resources.

The present economic problems of Italy are not to be solved by importing capital and thereby further increasing external indebtedness. Of course, I do believe that a country less developed than other countries around it can or must sometimes allow such imports for a time. But the ultimate solution to the problem is to accelerate the process of development inside the country. Efficiency is what is needed, and to that aim partially restoring the market economy might help.

Commentary

Diether H. Hoffmann

My contribution centers on a particular detail of the German economic system. With the exception of Sweden, there are only a few countries which have trade unions and corporate management sharing responsibility in industrial and economic enterprises. Besides Germany, one thinks of Austria and Israel.

After World War II, the unions became involved in corporate ownership, expanding their interest from simply seeing that wages were raised and kept at adequate levels. Their philosophy was that it is not enough to keep wages at an adequate level, but that it is also necessary to see to it that the spending of wages is influenced. In this new capacity, the successes of the trade unions are not lessened by low profits if their enterprises render services which they consider to be in their long-run interest. With this spirit and philosophy in mind, the German trade unions established a large holding organization and an insurance group, a bank, a travel agency, a book club, and a publishing house, which, incidentally, publishes the German edition of Professor Samuelson's book. The housing and development group owned by the trade unions is the biggest such group in the country; since 1950 it has built more than 400,000 units. It presently owns about 300,000 units. It is active in developing new settlements, city centers, hospitals, schools, universities, and commercial centers. The enlargement of the university of Bettingham, for instance, was one of its major achievements; so was one of the largest housing projects in Germany, with 10,000 units. At the present time, it is managing construction of the new congress center in Berlin.

Now I would like to make just a few remarks about the bank with which I am associated. We are one of the four banks in Germany involved in financing throughout the country. At the end of last year we had total assets of 22 billion Deutsche marks and equity of 1 billion Deutsche marks. To show how active we are, we now plan to open a branch in New York. What is our philosophy? We are partners in a market system. We work in that system with a special orientation toward the interest of the consumer. Our housing group is trying to raise the standard of housing, consistent with our belief that you cannot leave housing to builders who are interested only in making a profit; we have to have certain social standards which ensure the provision of adequate housing. Our insurance group was established and is still running on the principle of keeping fair premiums in the insurance business. We in the bank are trying to introduce new saving schemes. We are known for quoting the lowest rate for consumer loans, and are trying to help reserve jobs in companies which are endangered by mismanagement.

Now, I have just a few words on the role of profit in our companies. We are profit oriented; we are cost conscious; our pricing is market oriented because we consider profit to be a yardstick in achieving our goals in an economical manner. We are interested in profits to ensure the growth and future of our operations. However, we and our shareholders accept certain limitations on profits in the interest of the general public, the consumer, and the worker. We have only a small share of the market in which we deal; but by setting examples of social responsibility, we are in a position to influence the behavior of our competitors. One should not forget the impact that trade unions have had, by running and owning companies of this size, on the general climate and atmosphere of business in our country—an achievement which cannot be accounted for by measure of market share alone.

Let me conclude by remarking that in a society which depends on profits for efficient resource allocation, an unjust distribution of these resources may result. Therefore, societal limits must be set for profits. They can be set by competition; but since we know that competition does not work in all instances, limits must sometimes be imposed on an industry by examples set by others. That is what we are trying to do.

5 The Future of the Market System: A Round-table Discussion

Editor's Note: *The final session of the third series of The John Diebold Lectures was a round-table discussion of the future prospects for the market system. Four participants led off the discussion, with each focusing on what, from his vantage point, are the crucial elements on which this future depends.*

Commentary

Thornton F. Bradshaw

Probably more than any single group in America, today's businessmen are caught in a classic dilemma of change. Our basic stock in trade has been adaptability and a sense of realism—a capacity to adjust rapidly to new circumstances and a stubborn refusal to delude ourselves into believing that things are other than they are. The genius of the American free enterprise system has been its unceasing determination to look for what is coming next—to stop making buggy whips when the horseless carriage comes down the pike—to try something new that suits the fluctuations of the market.

Well, today we are caught up in larger currents of change than business has ever experienced in this country—and our response has too often been anything but flexible and innovative.

Looking around, we see massive problems: inflation, unemployment, pollution, wasteful use of resources and brutal competition for those that are left, and, of course, a whole range of festering issues grouped under the heading of economic and social injustice.

As realists we cannot deceive ourselves into thinking the solutions to these problems will not have an impact on us. We know they will. Moreover, we know that the role of government in the big decisions in economic as well as social affairs *must* increase because many critical matters have clearly gone beyond the capability of the marketplace to create solutions on a purely economic basis. I am speaking of problems that are inherently massive, with obviously serious consequences for the nation, and with lead times too great to permit the normal signal and response mechanism of the market to function in an orderly and timely manner. This much seems to me obvious.

Yet too many businessmen continue to reject the obvious. Too many, to judge by their speeches and other public comments, seem to think that not only will the problems disappear through some mysterious process but, if ignored long enough, the government itself will also disappear. Too many of us, in other words, are engaged in building a wall of negativism between business and the major social movements in the country and thereby isolating ourselves from the mainstream process of democratic decision making. I think this is a mistake. I think we need to be involved, and not simply as reluctant objects of government regulatory decisions, our actions directed by those who have only a shallow understanding of the economic realities and an often hostile regard for the whole enterprise system.

The question that faces America today is not whether we will have a mixed economy, a blending of public and private initiative, but what kind of mix it should be. I believe that there is a strong future for the market system in the country, but only if we who understand that system best can make the case with logic and force, and only if we are willing to acknowledge that government has a growing role in the economic system that must be shaped rather than fought. I am not asking for more government involvement in business per se, what I am suggesting is that the enterprise system cannot function properly without the right *kind* of government intervention—at the right time and in the right degree. For example, after 2 years of watching the halting and largely ineffectual efforts of government to deal with the energy issue, it seems more clear to me than ever that the country needs establishment of goals for energy planning on a national scale. And since energy pervades the economy, I think that by extension we need some kind of national economic planning as well.

There is surely ample reason to be concerned about the concept of national economic planning. Substituting the planning mechanism for the working of the market does inject the political process deeply into the areas that have traditionally been decided by consumer preference. And yet it seems to me that such arguments ignore the fact that national planning of a not very satisfactory kind is *already* a reality in this country, and that it exists not because of the machinations of power-hungry politicians but because we *need* it. The job of business at this point, in my opinion, is to contribute what we can to the development of a much better system of national planning than we now have. Whether we can preserve or restore the full vigor of the enterprise system in a government-dictated framework of operation is an open question at the moment. In any case, we must try.

I will use energy as an example, since it is the industry with which I am most familiar and because it also happens to be at the cutting edge of the effort to shape our mixed economy for the decades ahead. Petroleum is really a test case in the sense that it is the first of the competitive industries to face the possibility of permanent price and investment control in times other than war. The fate of my industry, good or bad, could well point the way for the rest of our enterprise system, whether toward continued freedom to innovate and grow or toward imprisonment in a sort of stagnating bureaucracy.

First, what are the areas in which I believe that government intervention in the energy business is necessary? And what form should the involvement take?

The starting place is clearly the establishment of a national energy policy, something the oil industry has been calling for since well before the Arab oil embargo of 1973-1974. The details have become familiar through dull repetition: we have called for measures that would conserve our indigenous supplies of oil and gas and other forms of fuel, that would encourage and facilitate rapid development of new domestic supplies of energy, and that would reduce this country's dependency on insecure foreign energy to a practical minimum—the level, in other words, that would permit us to regain a reasonable measure of energy independence.

The government should stipulate that by 1985 the United States will be no more than, say, 25 percent dependent for our energy on outside sources compared to 17.5 percent last year, and establish policies consistent with such a goal. Once that goal is established, the industry can start to adjust its pattern of investment and development to meet it. But if we were to rely entirely on the market to signal investments required to meet energy goals 9 years in the future, the signals would come too late. It is not that the government is somehow smarter than private entrepreneurs or superior in a philosophical sense, but government *is* obliged to give the country long-range directives and positioned to do it. Business is not. It's that simple.

Another reason for government intervention in the energy business is that the industry is simply not capable of achieving certain objectives that are clearly vital to the well-being of the nation. These are gaps in the private enterprise mechanism which the government alone can bridge.

For example, if it is considered necessary as part of the whole energy complex that a certain amount of oil be produced from shale, then we have to face the fact that private enterprise cannot do the job unassisted. The investment costs are stunning—probably $1 billion for a 50,000-barrel-a-day plant. At $11 a barrel, the present price of new oil is far below the level we would have to get for shale oil to pay that kind of front-end cost and still turn an acceptable profit. The inadequacy of ordinary market forces to produce a supply of shale oil means that the government will have to specify the industry's production objectives, clear away the environmental obstacles, underwrite the investment cost, and support the price of the product.

A third area in which I believe government involvement is absolutely essential is preparation for the next generation of fuels, those which will gradually replace gas and oil. This transition will be in full force around the turn of the twenty-first century, and the alternative fuels will probably be solar and nuclear fusion.

The problem here is that there is no way that our industry can anticipate energy requirements of 30 or 40 years from now. And even if we were able to look that far into the future, our capital resources are completely inadequate to finance the massive research program that would be required. Our company cannot obtain the kind of money needed, for example, to mount a meaningful attack on the fusion breakthrough problem—probably hundreds of millions of dollars. And even if we could, we could hardly ask our shareholders to wait decades for their return while the research proved out and became profitable. The enterprise system does not allow for that kind of long-term investment, so the answer is obviously a government-funded research program in exotic fuels.

Here again, what I am suggesting is *not* an abdication of the enterprise system to government, but a redesign of the public-private working relationship to take into account demands on our economic system that we simply have not had to cope with up to this point in history.

Economist and social critic Robert Heilbroner, an advocate of centralized planning, thinks coercive controls will be needed. Commenting on this aspect of national economic planning in a recent *New York Times* article, he wrote: "It is entirely possible that a given plan will include tax changes as part of its means-ends machinery: tax incentives for industries to invest in ways that are congenial to the plan: tax penalties for industries that do not." "Very stringent controls or prohibitions," he adds, "might have to be imposed on industry and household alike. . . ."

I agree with him—to a degree. For example, there will continue to be a need to depress energy demand, particularly the use of oil. I do not see how the market can accomplish this goal by itself, even if prices were freed tomorrow. Therefore the government must mandate minimum mileage for cars; the government must impose a tax on horsepower, penalizing powerful cars; the government must facilitate and encourage the use of insulation; and so forth. The government, in brief, must interfere with things people would normally do in order to reduce energy demand to an acceptable level.

Next, the government must provide certain additives to the economic system if we are to meet our energy goals. Shale oil, as I have pointed out, is a particular problem. It is not economical and we foresee no circumstances under which it will *be* economical in competition with conventional sources of oil and other forms of energy.

If you leave production of shale to the market alone, there will not be any, or at any rate, very little. If the government says we must have a certain amount by 1985 or 1990, then the government must make it possible through guaranteed loans to help build the first 5 to 10 plants, through price supports to compensate for high production costs and possibly through wholesale purchases of the shale oil itself as a guaranteed market.

Next, there must be a program of continuing protection of U.S. energy companies from foreign producers. If this industry is to spend hundreds of billions of dollars in the next 15 years to achieve energy independence—a government goal—then the companies need assurance that the government will protect them if there is an energy embargo or if the OPEC cartel breaks and floods the market with oil at $5 a barrel.

In short, the government must set goals and create and police standards, using tax and legislative authorities as necessary. But Heilbroner and I—and Galbraith and I—part company on the question of price controls. I have had a long and painful experience with price controls, and I can assure you that in the case of the oil industry at least, they have been wholly counterproductive.

Achieving cooperation between the public and private sectors has been made very difficult by the special circumstances in which we have been functioning ever since the Arab oil embargo made energy a *cause célèbre*. The post-Watergate atmosphere of public suspicion has engulfed all of our major institutions, including the Congress, the Presidency, and big business.

When the air has cleared, I believe that my industry and corporate capitalism generally can make a convincing case for their continued existence on two principal grounds. First, the market economy is the most democratic instrument for human material progress that has ever been invented. If planning can improve economic conditions, I am for it. But any centralized planning scheme that would contrive to limit the individual citizen's right to buy or sell would fatally compromise the economic vigor of this country. Liberals and conservatives alike must reject the ultimate consequences of bureaucratizing fundamental entrepreneurial and management functions.

Second, relatively autonomous business enterprise is an important check on the power of government, contributing, as Irving Kristol has said, "to a general diffusion of power . . . which creates the 'space' in which individual liberty can survive and prosper."

In fact, when you get right down to it, the second argument for the survival of the market may be more important to the long-range interests of democracy than the first. As *Time* magazine recently noted, "There is no alternative to capitalism that credibly promises both wealth and liberty." A valuable thought, I would say, for the bicentennial year.

Commentary

McGeorge Bundy

First, I should confess to all of you that I have worked unrepentantly in the nonprofit sector all my life, and if you bury the profit sector, I probably ought to go back to New York to check the Ford Foundation portfolio. On second thought, perhaps I ought to stay here and help Henry Rosovsky because we are sitting in a tribute to the profit system. This building was in the design stages when I lived in Cambridge. The design was not hard; I had a part in it myself. But making it happen was the action of a great entrepreneur, and the funds with which he made it happen came from a Polaroid camera. So there is a relationship between nonprofit organization and the world of profit, and that is my excuse for taking some of your time.

Let me say first that I agree with a great deal of what has just been said. I do think that many in this country, especially businessmen and conservatives of all descriptions waste a great deal of time trying to turn the clock back. All it does is jam the machinery. I do think that politics and the political process decide the great goals, and also the goals within a subfield as large and important as energy. I also believe, and I think this was a thread that went through everything that was said here, that a relatively honest and open marketplace is an essential part of a good society for a whole variety of reasons. It is very hard to conceive of the kind of life that any of us would want to live without the openness and right of choice that the economic marketplace provides. Having said that, I have to add that I am not impressed by most arguments that I have heard in favor of any particular pattern, role, locus, size, or entitlement to profit in the marketplace; that to me was the instructive lesson of the remarks thus far.

What we were hearing earlier is that in the opinion of people who are students of many different kinds of societies, no one particular pattern of investment or profit is in itself indispensible in a relatively honest and open market. If I heard Mr. Carli correctly, he was expressing cautious hope about a kind of enterprise that would not be described by the American Chamber of Commerce as a free enterprise. If I heard Professor Lundberg correctly, he too was cautious but thoughtfully hopeful that the traditional processes of adjustment, compromise, and political goal setting in Sweden would accommodate a dramatic change in the source and destiny of profit without destroying an extraordinarily effective market economy. The same thing was said about Germany, and suggested, at least in theoretical terms, by Professor Bergson in his account of the failed society (failed in market terms) in the Soviet Union.

My next point is that unfairness and inequality (and I would add unemployment and inflation, the twin devils of the specifically current economic scene) can be attacked in ways that do not have to lower the efficiency of any particular productive or market process. That again is a lesson, as was indicated earlier, of the Swedish case. Concerning Mr. Bradshaw's remarks, I am sure that he knows as well as I do that there are other ways of putting a cost on, or deriving a tax from, either the producer or the consumer of energy, and that those ways are not in themselves inconsistent with the operation of a market process. The process of reducing inequality and unfairness in our society, which to me should be one of the fundamental and proper political goals of America, is one which can be addressed without attacking the marketplace. I will not go into detail on that because some of the best work on it that I have seen was done by Arthur Okun in lectures delivered here two years ago.

I think we also heard it said, and I believe, that savings and investment can be generated in many ways, and that no one pattern should be sanctified, since to do that is indeed a flagrant indulgence in Professor Whitehead's fallacy of misplaced concreteness. We heard from Professor Lundberg that managers do not care where money comes from. I think he is right. Some of you may have seen predictions that we are headed toward pension-fund socialism right here in the United States. And Mr. Bradshaw can tell you better than I how much government encouragement to investment would be applied by Vice President Rockefeller's proposal for energy independence. I do not think Mr. Rockefeller has been accused of intending to destroy the free enterprise system. So I take it that there are lots of different ways of generating funds for investment, and I think again of those who were describing particular societies and offering illustrations of different ways. If we had been able to get Dean Rosovsky to join the discussion, he would have been able to give illuminating examples from the extraordinarily interesting and quite different case in Japan.

Having suggested that defenses of particular profit systems are suspect, let me add that I believe that operating effectiveness depends both on the existence of a market and of some kind of process by which effective management capacity is generated and allowed to do its job. The same thing is true of investment. You can do it in many ways but only if there is a will to do it. A society which prefers current consumption to investment will in the end pay the price, or its children will. We are in some danger of that here. There are devastating examples of this in other countries, which have been referred to in earlier discussions. If your processes do not confront the market challenge with effectiveness, you will fail. You will confront the kinds of difficulties, to cite one example from earlier discussions, that are faced in Italy. What makes for good management is not a question which connects automatically to profit, and that I think is an error of judgment which is frequent in the United States. I do not think that it is the quality of the effort for immediate maximization or even long-term maximization of profit as such that is the one unfailing sign or test of an effective economic management unit. I do not think that is the lesson of experience in the United States itself, and I do not think it is the lesson of experience in Japan, Germany, or Sweden. I do not believe that we get to the root of what makes a good company or a good management unit by starting from the question of how profits are generated. I think we have to go to questions of sociology, culture, or the way in which human beings organize themselves. I think rewards for effective management are terribly important, but there are rewards other than profit.

What I am trying to say is that as you organize an economic order, national or international, you do want to look hard at the ways and means by which a market is kept relatively honest and open; you do want to look at the ways by which a national will to save and invest is created or sustained and made operative; you do need to look at how the market and managing capacity interconnect; and you do need to concern yourself, as Mr. Bradshaw said, with underlying political purposes and the political processes by which those purposes are made effective. But you should look with skepticism upon any proposition that a particular pattern in our own economic organization or that of any other country should be given an automatic priority or approval. That applies whether we are talking about business ideology or the intractable Phillips' curve.

Commentary

Gabriel Hauge

I am delighted to join this discussion on a very considerable problem of our time: how we organize ourselves to get the world's work done. I will draw on experience gained from three career vantage points. First, my brief and junior participation in the academic world, where primary concerns were relevance and engagement. Second, in government, where enormous frustration characterized the complex decision-making process. Finally, my years in the business world, where we try to cope with a great deal of uncertainty.

I want to touch three or four topics, but first, a word about the language barrier in this discussion. Take, for example, a word as basic as *profits*. I do not use the word myself; I prefer *earnings*. It provides a clearer picture of what the bottom line means, and it is not blurred by the acrimonious debate that over the years has surrounded the term *profits*.

Market system, to offer another example, is a good phrase, certainly better than *capitalism*. People understand what it means. I am aware that opinion polls report low marks for business, which is a synonym for the market system, and for businessmen in general. That is probably natural at a time of rising prices, stubborn unemployment, reduced overtime, and revelations of the transgressions of some private-sector leaders. I am also aware, however, that these same polls register low marks for government, for academics, and for most everybody else.

These less than shining judgments, however, do not reflect basic hostility toward our economic system. Organized labor, for example, is not dedicated to the radical transformation of the market system. There is no political party here, such as in the United Kingdom, whose purpose is to dominate the private sector. The strength of private business here is a primary concern of all.

When I ask about Great Britain's economy, for example, my questions mainly concern the morale of the nation's entrepreneurs. Do they possess the dynamism which, under intelligent and forward-looking government policy, can generate economic growth needed to make a mixed economy work?

Our own economy does not face such basic internal division. In the presidential race, I find no one challenging the market system under which we prosper. Every once in a while Fred Harris digresses into his populist philosophy, but then I do not think he represents a serious challenge. There is a good deal of consensus on the merits of the market system. The point has been stated before, but I think it is worth noting again.

Profits or earnings determine your standing in the market system league, and that is fundamental. It is more than a piece of blue ribbon, more than your name at the top of a totem pole or a performance record. It is the fundamental aspect of the market system. There are rewards. They are related not only to salary levels and fringe benefits but also to the corporate performance which earnings reflect. Our country is not so rich that it can forget efficiency. And while this is a very hard doctrine for people because it connotes work measurement and all the demanding things that productivity implies, I believe it is commonly accepted that we have to be efficient. Efficiency is measured in the international markets. When, for example, our goods cannot compete in real terms with those of foreign producers, we are not efficient. I am talking about a system that is accepted and that can be made to work better.

There is also a general belief, despite some of the headlines lately, that we enjoy a reasonably responsive and well-functioning financial system, allocating a great part of the country's capital and credit resources, other than that which the various levels of government appropriate through taxes or borrowing. Access to financial markets is determined by the quality of earnings, the strength of balance sheets, and the talent of management. The alternative, a state-determined allocation of credit, was suggested in this country last year when the chairman of the House Banking and Currency Committee introduced a bill that provided for credit allocation. The bill still has not cleared his committee.

Challenges facing the market system clearly include unjustified, anticompetitive elements. Fear of monopoly and oligopoly in product and labor markets have generated an antitrust tradition in this country which seeks to keep the market system competitive. But government interventions have led to all sorts of rigidities. Hendrik Houthakker here at Harvard has made a list of these interventions in agriculture, transportation, and energy that runs for pages. It gives an insight into what happens when we shift economic decision making from the market to the Congress or government agencies. Charitably judged, the record is mixed. Hopefully, we will learn from experience.

Other unfinished items of business for the market system are what I alluded to earlier—good jobs and honest dollars, the issues of inflation and unemployment. They are stubborn problems. The economic analysis, let alone the solution, is not yet agreed upon. Neo-Keynesianism does not seem to be the answer; public stabilization policies have themselves become a source of instability. Exactly what will deal effectively with the problem is still a little beyond our reach. Part of the trouble, in my view, stems from the fact that we have believed for some years that if we do not get the last billion dollars of GNP out of the productive mechanism, we are somehow failing.

I hope we have learned that what we must seek is a "cruising speed" for the economy. If that proves to be below full utilization, then we must provide supplementary ways of dealing with those elements, particularly of the labor force, that are not fully engaged.

This lays a heavy burden on monetary and fiscal policies. We are still searching for ways to control M-1 and the other money-supply indicators. Monetary control has been likened to walking a dog on a very long leash; we have, indeed, found how difficult it can be. In the field of fiscal policy, we have learned in my town of New York that, as the book of Ecclesiastes puts it, "Be not made a beggar by banqueting upon borrowing." The lesson applies also to our state and yours. We simply have to pull up our fiscal socks and pay for more of what we think we want in the public sector. If not, we will find the capital markets for an increasing number of public entities clamped shut.

Society's noneconomic objectives, such as environmental matters, also require careful definition. After an initial surge that tried to compensate for years of neglect, the debate has sobered up to one of "pace and price." Also under the heading of noneconomic objectives are questions of job satisfaction and quality of life. Attention here is long delayed.

There persists as well the question of distribution of income. My own view is simple enough: equal rights to earn unequal incomes. This places a great deal of emphasis on both government programs and private efforts, but it is, I believe, the fundamental way to improve income distribution. Beyond that, we need to develop some kind of family assistance program or a negative income tax approach to consolidate the piecemeal efforts we now employ in addressing the problems of the poor and disadvantaged.

There are many other things to say in this regard, but let one concluding remark suffice. A great challenge confronts the academic community—to give us more tools, more analyses capable of coping with some of the problems I have cited. Fortunately, I think I see some hopeful signs forthcoming.

I have, for example, been particularly heartened by some of the academic inquiries dealing with the lag in research and development expenditures in the United States. It is important that we understand the reasons why they have been lagging and how we can arrest the lag. I am also very much interested in the attempts to fashion post-Keynesian principles that will provide policy guidance for economies other than those characterized by large-scale, prolonged subpar performance. I have looked at what the radical economists say in this regard. They highlight unsolved problems on our agenda, but I do not believe they have outlined an alternative suitable for America.

In the business sector, it seems to me, we are faced with three challenges. The first is doing the job. Our companies exist by sufferance of our customers and the electorate. We are committed to the risks of the marketplace, and we will succeed only if we indeed build a better mousetrap and price it right. That is what the market is about, what efficiency is about, what earnings are about. The sanction is clear enough. We understand and accept it.

Recently we have been confronted with a growing list of demands which we in the private sector should accomplish. A good deal of it we can do, but some of it is beyond our capability. The fundamental response of businessmen to these challenges is the kind of superior performance that grows out of quality and service, a governing attitude that the public be served, cost-benefit investment, more care about the people we work with than anybody else could give, and commitment to being good corporate citizens.

Second, we need to tell the story. It never ceases to amaze me how our fellow citizens take the market system for granted. The capacity of American business to build a car and put it in the showroom down the street, to transport petroleum from under the North Sea and turn it into gasoline at the station on the corner, to manufacture agricultural chemicals that multiply food production, to conjure up fibers from gas and oil derivatives for clothing in the shops, to create miracle drugs for our hospitals—all this is considered normal, natural, and effortless, and is as much taken for granted as the rising of the sun. As we all know, it is not quite that effortless. Nor is it a matter of ideology or philosophy. It is a matter of results and facts, and we should not tamper mindlessly with the system that makes it all possible.

Finally, keep the faith. The business leadership which operates in the marketplace bears a heavy burden of suspicion and guilt by association because some members of the fraternity have knowingly broken the laws of the land. Breach of faith justly visits the wrath of the community on the faithless, but unjustly on many of the faithful as well. Keeping the faith is neither a plain nor simple matter. But this much is clear, a market system must be the place for honest competition. If not, we lack the right to claim that it should be permitted to function. It remains our responsibility to embody standards of integrity that will radiate from our companies and serve as a beacon across the land.

Commentary

D. Quinn Mills

This marks the close of the second day of this conference. By my count I am the sixteenth person to speak, so there is not a great deal left to be said, particularly from the point of view of the economist. I recall a story which is not new but may be particularly appropriate at this stage. It is about three people: a physician, an engineer, and an economist who were discussing which of their professions was the oldest. The physician began by saying, "Certainly the medical profession is the oldest of the three, because the first book of Genesis describes how the Lord took a rib from Adam to create Eve. "That," he said, "was clearly a surgical procedure, and established the ancient lineage of the profession." The engineer commented that that was correct and that indeed the medical profession was a very old profession, but he reminded the two other gentlemen that in an earlier part of the book of Genesis the Lord created heaven and earth out of chaos. "That was clearly an engineering procedure" he said, "and established engineering as the oldest profession." The economist said, "Yes, both are honorable and ancient professions, but after all," he asked them, "who do you think created the chaos?"

I think many of you at this stage must have no doubt as to who created the chaos. And I do not think that there is much that I can do to summarize what has gone before. What I thought I might do is approach from a somewhat different perspective a question that is before us. Profit is a key element of our free market system. If the essence of the system is decentralized decision making in individual enterprise, then profits provide both the incentive and the means for this system to operate. One can see from a brief look at the numbers, however, that profits have not been doing well in the United States. Profits as a percentage of national income (this is a commonly used measure of profits before taxes, including depreciation allowances and an inventory evaluation adjustment) have declined from 14 percent in 1950 to about 8½ percent in 1975. Profits in 1975 as a percentage of national income are at the same level as in the period 1910 to 1930.

However, compensation of employees gives quite a different picture. In 1900, compensation of employees was approximately 55 percent of national income; in 1950, 65 percent; in 1975, 76 percent. The growth in employee compensation has come largely from declines in rental income and the income of proprietors, and this reflects in part the decline of the small proprietary sector in the economy. But gains have been made in employee compensation in this century, not in corporate profits. And there is, I think, a long-term profit squeeze in our future. We in the United States think of Western Europe and Japan as moving into high-compensation, low-profit economies. As one looks

121

into the future, the pressure of reduced rates of productivity and low current levels of capital investment can only accentuate movement in this direction in the United States as well.

Now, I would like to look at this problem from a somewhat different perspective. We are fortunate that no major or very influential element of our society is currently challenging the very existence of profits or private ownership. This is not so in other industrialized countries. Fundamental challenges come from the Marxist parties and from the Marxist-allied trade union movement. Were this to be the case in the United States, or were it to become the case in the future, then those of us considering the future of the market system and of profits would have to be less certain of a favorable outcome. In the United States, the trade union movement as a whole supports the profit system. In its defense of American capitalism, the U.S. labor movement is isolated from trade union movements abroad. President Meany of the AFL-CIO a few years ago set forth the philosophy of the trade union movement in a speech to the ministers of labor of the governments which comprised the Organization of American States. I think it is important to note that these comments were made not to an American audience but to a foreign one. Mr. Meany's comments at that time included the following statements:

American organized labor operating under our free system has made progress over the years. While we are by no means satisfied, perhaps we will never be satisfied, we believe that the opportunities for progress for wage earners under our system are greater than under any other system recorded in history. . . . Organized labor in America is part and parcel of the American economic system. We accept without question the right of management to manage with reasonable consideration, of course, for the rights of workers to a fair share of the wealth produced. We accept without question the right of management to adequate compensation for its efforts. We accept without question the right of the investor for a return on his investment in an enterprise. We accept the practice of allocating some portion of the wealth produced by business or corporations to technical research necessary for future development. Under this system, the only reasonable difference of opinion between American labor and American management is over the share the worker receives of the wealth that he helps to produce. That, of course, is the simple basic reason for trade union instrumentality. We want to have a say as to what the fair share of the worker will be.

In effect, the unions in the United States support the profits of the free market system in the hope of taking a substantial amount of those profits for the worker. I think that the statistics I cited earlier show that they have not done a bad job of it. Mr. Meany is not, however, nor is the labor movement in the United States, an uncritical supporter of the daily activities of the business community or the American government. About the business community, Mr. Meany is reported to have said, "The history of modern American business discloses that time after time it has had to be rescued from crises brought about by its own insensate greed." And the criticisms of government policy voiced by the AFL-CIO are so frequent and so strident that they require no special citation here. Yet this criticism is not of the system itself, but of its operations.

The position of the American trade union movement is in contrast to that of most labor movements abroad. Basically, European trade unions have sought to advance the entire working class by transforming the total society. European labor movements place a much greater emphasis on achievement of substantial change in the social system through political ends than does labor in the United States. The difference of philosophy between Communist elements in the European labor movement and the American labor is clear from a glance at the ideology of the CGT (the General Confederation of Labor) in France. The CGT is communist-affiliated and represents approximately 2 million of the 3 million unionized French workers. The CGT's objective is to end the capitalist system, and it maintains that its goals and those of capitalist management are fundamentally opposed. A collective bargaining agreement, it says, may be viewed as no more than an armistice in the class struggle between labor and management, a struggle in which there will be no final peace until labor is victorious.

What does the future hold? A change in the attitude of American labor toward free enterprise and American business would, in my judgment, fundamentally alter the political and social context of American business operations. It might well cause policy changes in government which would be inimical to the profit system. Could such a change occur? I think that perhaps it could. There is no immediate evidence of it, but it is certainly a matter worth considering. These are very important matters. One of Harvard's distinguished economists remarked that "history abounds with examples of countries that find themselves rich or poor by their choice of economic policy." Mr. Slichter did not have in mind short-term fiscal and monetary policy, but rather the longer-term decisions which affect the form of an economic system and its level of investment and innovation. There is evidence that concern is developing abroad over the accumulating impact of high consumption and low profits. This concern goes beyond logical squabblings; it is a practical problem for practical men, of whatever ideological persuasion.

Let me cite an example. Prime Minister Wilson of Great Britain began his book of memoirs by describing the record of the labor government, which was in power from 1964 to 1970, with a quotation from Mr. Bevin's (a long-time leftist leader of the Labor Party) last speech in the House of Commons: "I would describe the central problem falling upon representative government in the Western world as how to persuade the people to forego immediate satisfaction in order to build up the economic resources of the country." This statement was made in 1959. In recent weeks in 1976, Mr. Wilson (again Prime Minister) has introduced a budget intended to forego satisfactions in order to attempt to rebuild the economic resources of Britain. One wonders if it can be done, or if it is not perhaps too late. An American, I think, must thank his lucky stars that he has thus far been spared these hard choices and the great risks which the British now face. We do, of course, wish them well.

We in the United States must not be complacent. The profit system is under considerable criticism, and it is subject to great public suspicion. Furthermore, too unstable an economy is not a good environment for free enterprise (for business and profit), either economically or politically. In recent years, we have gambled with the range of toleration of this economy for instability. Fortunately, we appear to have survived intact. Free markets and competition in the United States remain vigorous despite some exceptions in certain industries. The source of this vigor is increasing competition, which continues to result from the expansion of markets, particularly the development of competition on a worldwide basis. There continue to be improvements in transportation, products, and production processes. These factors do not appear to be improving as fast now as they have in the immediate past, but they continue to be important influences. I would like to quote Professor Slichter again: "The holders of the belief that competition is declining look back to an imaginary age when the country was made up of many thousands of small concerns, all vigorously competing with one another. As a matter of fact, these conditions never existed." Instead of looking back, we must attempt to make the best of what is possible and recognize that profits do have an important role in preserving this free system.

List of Contributors and Commentators

Kenneth J. Arrow
James B. Conant University Professor
Harvard University

Abram Bergson
George F. Baker Professor of Economics
Harvard University

Thornton F. Bradshaw
President
Atlantic Richfield Company

McGeorge Bundy
President
The Ford Foundation

Guido Carli
President
Ente Einaudi

Benjamin M. Friedman
Associate Professor of Economics
Harvard University

Arthur W. Harrigan
Executive Vice President, Finance
International Paper Company

C. Lowell Harriss
Professor of Economics
Columbia University

Gabriel Hauge
Chairman
Manufacturers Hanover Trust Company

Diether H. Hoffmann
Member of the Managing Board
Bank für Gemeinwirtschaft

Erik Lundberg
Professor of Economics
The Stockholm School of Economics

D. Quinn Mills
Professor of Business Administration
Harvard University

Russell E. Palmer
Managing Partner and Chief Executive Officer
Touche, Ross & Company

Henry Rosovsky
Walter S. Baker Professor of Economics and Dean
   of the Faculty of Arts and Sciences
Harvard University

Paul A. Samuelson
Institute Professor
Massachusetts Institute of Technology

Eli Shapiro
Chairman of the Finance Committee and Director
The Travellers Insurance Companies

Peter Temin
Professor of Economics
Massachusetts Institute of Technology

Henry C. Wallich
Member
Board of Governors of the Federal Reserve System

About the Editor

Benjamin M. Friedman is associate professor of economics at Harvard University, where he teaches macroeconomics and monetary theory and policy. His recent research has focused on public-policy implications of financial markets and the influence of financial markets on macroeconomic activity, including such topics as the determination of long-term interest rates, and financial impacts on capital formation.

Dr. Friedman received the A.B., A.M., and Ph.D. degrees in economics from Harvard University; during his graduate study he was a Junior Fellow of the Society of Fellows. He also received the M.Sc. in economics and politics from King's College, Cambridge, where he studied as a Marshall Scholar.

Dr. Friedman is the author of *Economic Stabilization Policy* and has published papers on monetary economics, macroeconomics, and economic policy. He is currently serving as an associate editor of the *Journal of Monetary Economics,* as a member of the Brookings Panel on Economic Activity, as an academic consultant to the Federal Reserve Board, and as the program director for monetary economics and financial markets at the National Bureau of Economic Research.